# 52
# WEEKS OF WRITING

Author journal and planner

## ALSO BY MARIËLLE S. SMITH

*52 Weeks of Writing Author Journal and Planner, Vol. II: Get out of your own way and become the writer you're meant to be*

*365 Days of Gratitude Journal: Commit to the life-changing power of gratitude by creating a sustainable practice*

*Get Out of Your Own Way: A 31-Day Tarot Challenge for Writers and Other Creatives*
(also available in Spanish and Dutch)

*Tarot for Creatives: 21 Tarot Spreads to (Re)Connect to Your Intuition and Ignite that Creative Spark*
(also available in Spanish, French, and Dutch)

*Fleshing Out the Narrative: A 31-Day Tarot and Journal Challenge for Writers*

*Set Yourself Up for Success: A 31-Day Tarot Challenge for Writers and Other Creatives*

*Seven Simple Spreads Book 1: Seven Simple Card Spreads to Unlock Your Creative Flow*

*Seven Simple Spreads Book 2: Seven Simple Card Spreads to Direct Your Creative Flow*

*Seven Simple Spreads Book 3: Seven Simple Card Spreads to Boost Your Confidence*

*Seven Simple Spreads Book 4: Seven Simple Card Spreads to Celebrate Your Creative Wins*

*Speak Your Truth: A 31-Day Tarot Challenge for Writers and Other Creatives*

*Step into Your Power: A 31-Day Tarot Challenge to Unleash Your Creative Potential*

## CO-WRITTEN UNDER THE PEN NAME HEATHER MACLEE

*Too Good to Be True?*

*Where There's a Will*

*There's a Way*

# 52
# WEEKS OF WRITING

VOL. I

Author journal and planner

Get out of your own way and become the writer you're meant to be

Mariëlle S. Smith

Copyright © 2019 by M.S. Wordsmith

All rights reserved.

No part of this book may be reproduced in any form or by any electronic or mechanical means, including information storage and retrieval systems, without written consent of the copyright holder except for the use of brief quotations in a book review.

ISBN 9781705421277

To everyone who told me to keep writing

# Introduction

Welcome to *52 Weeks of Writing*, a journal and planner for writers ready to get out of their own way so they can become the writers they are meant to be. I'm so glad you picked up a copy! This author journal and planner reflects everything I've learned over the past several years as a writing coach and writer. All my clients' struggles and victories (as well as my own) have seeped into these pages.

Coaches don't come cheap. No matter how much we could use one, it isn't always an option. While no journal or planner can stand in for an actual living, breathing writing coach who will work with you one on one, *52 Weeks of Writing* is my attempt to bridge the gap as best as I can.*

Who is this author journal and planner for?

When someone first asked me who I was developing *52 Weeks of Writing* for, my immediate response was 'Not for the faint of heart'. At the time, I meant it as a joke, but the more I thought about it, the more I realised it actually sums up my coaching clients quite nicely. None of them came to me looking for someone to hold their hand and tell them it was all going to be just fine.

On the contrary. What all my clients have in common is that they are fed up with themselves and how their writing isn't progressing, at least not in the way or at the pace they want it to. The reason they come to me is because they need someone to ask the right questions—which are never the easy ones—while providing them with a safe space where they can chew on their answers. Although it doesn't make the ride any smoother, with me by their side, it's just that much easier for them to dig deeper and unravel whatever uncomfortable truths about their writing practice need to be brought to the surface.

My aim for this author journal and planner is to provide that safe space in physical, or digital, form. The questions I ask my clients are here; what's different is that I'm not around to prod and poke any further whenever I sense you hold something back or are not honest with yourself. I'm also not here to keep you accountable. That, too, is up to you, and that's why I highly recommend you find yourself an accountability partner, if you don't already have one. You're always welcome to join me and my fellow writers in my Facebook group, The Accountable Wordsmiths, too.

Why a journal and planner in one?

To keep a long answer short: because planning alone will only get us so far. Planning ahead and then taking the time to sit with our results and ponder how they came to be, that's how we figure out not just patterns of behaviour, but also why these patterns keep showing up. Consistently keeping track of and thinking through what we are doing allows us to truly get to the bottom of our struggles. And that's where we need to get if we want to tackle them once and for all.

As I write these words, I'm sitting in my sea-view apartment on the coast of Cyprus, a small island in the middle of the Mediterranean Sea. Every day, I get to do what I love—I write, and I help other writers do the same. I have the most supportive partner and a community that believes in me a hundred per cent. To top it off, I've published eight books since September 2018. However, my life wasn't always like this. In fact, it looked nothing like it until quite recently.

I've been into yoga for the last eight years or so. With every new teacher I encountered, the same questions came up: How was my meditation practice? My breathing? Did I do any journaling? No. No, I did not. No meditation, no journaling, and, let's face it, I wasn't breathing properly either. I've embraced many yogic principles since I started doing yoga, but anything to do with sitting still, being mindful, and allowing thoughts to come? That I avoided at all costs.

We avoid things for a reason, and my reason was that I was afraid to uncover the truth about why I wasn't happy. With myself, my day job, my relationship, my writing, how my freelance business was doing. I kept telling myself I was content, and that being content was good enough. It took me years to figure out I wasn't even that: I was uncomfortably numb. I was at a The National concert with a friend in 2017 when I suddenly felt so alive I couldn't help but admit I felt mostly dead inside on other days.

That concert became my turning point. I bought a brand-new journal and I started writing. I've journaled before in my life, and it had always felt like a useless exercise. What's the point of putting pen to paper if it doesn't change anything? They say writing it down—like saying it aloud—makes it real, but we underestimate how easy it is to forget what we've spelled out. Especially when there's something at stake, like us not wanting to leave our uncomfortable comfort zones. This time, however, I was aware that just writing it down wouldn't get me anywhere. I was going to free write, to see what needed to come to the fore, and then I was going to reread and write about that. I was going to sit with what would come up, reflect on it, and deal with it. Again and again.

And so I did. Fast forward a couple of years, I quit my day job, I ended my relationship, and I moved countries to focus on my coaching, my editing, and my writing business and practice full-time. Now, I'm not saying I wouldn't have gotten to this point without my journaling, but I know one thing to be true: if I hadn't bought that journal the day after seeing The National and started journaling like I meant it, I wouldn't have gotten where I am now this fast. Which explains how this anti-journaler came to create a journal of her own. Because if I can do it, so can you.

As you will soon notice, quite a few questions in this author journal and planner come back every week. However, it's important—and I can't stress this enough—to sit with each question every single week before jotting down your answer. Don't rush through them just because they are the same as last week and the week before. They keep coming back for a reason, and that is to help you get to the root of whatever is in your way. I can't tell you how many times of writing down the exact same answer it took me to realise that, maybe, there was another layer to it (trust me, an awful lot of times). Or, how many weeks of the same question it took before I was ready to take that deep breath and acknowledge what I couldn't in the weeks before. You too will get there, but only if you're willing to put in the work and sit with the questions at hand. Consistently.

When I say 'sit with it', I mean it, too. Try not to answer any of these questions quickly, in between chores or jobs or social engagements. Carve out time each week, even more so for the quarterly check-ins, and tune in with yourself. This could mean doing some breathwork, putting on the right kind of music, making yourself a nice cuppa, whatever you need.

The more grounded you are when answering the questions in this journal and planner, the easier it will be for the real answer—the one you've been waiting for—to surface. It might take a few weeks or even months before you manage to peel away all the layers, but there's nowhere for the truth to hide once we stop running and start showing up for ourselves. It's only a matter of time, and I hope you can find the patience and discipline to grant yourself that time. You, and the writer you're meant to be, are worth it.

Mariëlle S. Smith

* Of course, if you come across something you can't solve by yourself as you work your way through this author journal and planner, please consider contacting a coach. If that is too far out of your comfort zone or you don't know where to start, drop me a line at marielle@mswordsmith.nl. At the very least, I can help you assess what you need and point you in the right direction.

# HOW TO WORK 52 WEEKS OF WRITING

*52 Weeks of Writing* consists of various elements. Some return every week, others each quarter, and again others only show up at the very start and / or end. Below, you will find a short overview of the different elements and what they're for in order of appearance.

- Clarity

The *Clarity* section comes back each quarter and aims to get you clear on what makes you tick as a writer and what is in the way of your goals and dreams.

- Goals

In the *Goals* section, we focus on your long-term goals. We start by where you see yourself in ten years, then in five years, three years, two, and so on. As you write down these goals, really try to visualise them. What will achieving them look like? How will it make you feel? How are you going to celebrate? The clearer you can envision yourself reaching your goals, the easier it will be to stay excited about them.

Your goals are not set in stone. They are meant to provide direction and focus, and can be adjusted at all times. This is why the author journal and planner checks in with your three-month to one-year goals each quarter. Perhaps you quickly realise that your one-year goal isn't feasible, because it means you need to get more done within six months than you can possibly pull off. Simply go back to the goals you've set and tweak where necessary.

Don't forget every writer has their own personal goals, so don't think about what others are doing or aiming for. What is reasonable for you? Some of us have the privilege to have all day to write, while others are lucky to carve out thirty minutes four days a week. Likewise, some writers will want to go with traditional publishing, while others prefer going indie. These different routes come with different steps to take, so make sure you reflect on those as well as you set your goals.

- Planning

The weekly *Planning* section is where you get to plan your week ahead and break down your bigger goals for the week into smaller pieces. If you have no idea what is realistic for you at this point, that's OK. You have fifty-two weeks to go, so there is ample opportunity to test your limits. Just start somewhere; you'll soon learn whether you need to ask more or less of yourself.

- Tracking

The weekly *Tracking* section is where you reflect on whether you achieved your weekly goal(s) and think of ways how to do better next time.

- Writing quotes and prompts

Every week starts with a writing quote to keep you inspired, and ends with a writing prompt or exercise designed to make you grow as a writer in all ways imaginable. Some prompts will help you train your writing muscle, others your author mindset. Some might be easy, while others will push you right out of your comfort zone, asking you to dig as deep as you dare and broaden your horizon as far as you can or want to at this time. All prompts and exercises are optional, so if you ever feel it's too much, don't force yourself through it. Simply come back another time.

- Reflecting

The quarterly *Reflecting* section invites you to think about how far you've come, what you've learned, and what you are most grateful for.

- Goal overview

The *Goal overview* at the end of the author journal and planner provides an overview of all your goals of the year, whether or not you achieved them, and the lessons you've learned.

Whether you want to update the *Goal overview* weekly, monthly, quarterly, or at the end of the year is entirely up to you, as long as you keep reflecting on your progress. There's a reason why this author journal and planner includes so many questions to ponder: if we don't sit with and look at where we've been and where we are now, we miss the opportunity to learn and improve and become the writers we were always meant to be.

# YOU READY?

# WEEK 1

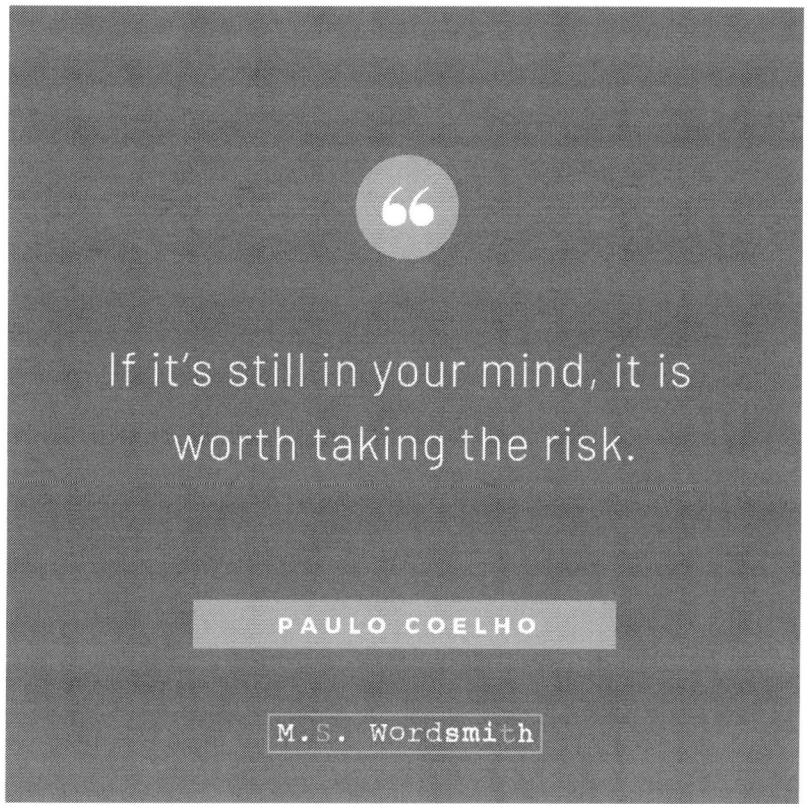

DATE: 21.3.2022

# CLARITY

When you first started writing, why were you called to write?

Es war ein Gefühl. Es lief Frank 4 im radio. und ich wusste plötzlich: Ich bin nicht hier, um in einem Hotel zu arbeiten. Ich bin hier, um zu schreiben.

When you first started writing, how did it make you feel?

Purposeful! On a mission.

Do you still feel like that when you write? If not, what has changed?

Yes!

# CLARITY

**What are your current struggles and roadblocks when it comes to writing?**

I don't take the time.
I don't take it serious.
I think: nobody will read it in the end. Is it worth the time?

**For each struggle and roadblock, can you determine which are internal or external?**

It's all internal

**For each struggle and roadblock, what do you think you need to overcome it?**

Ich müsste daran glauben, dass ich es nicht umsonst schreibe. Toll wäre es, wenn ich wüsste, dass es ein Erfolg wird. Veröffentlicht in einem guten Verlag mit vielen, vielen Lesern

# GOALS

**Where do you want to be ten years from now? How are you going to celebrate?**

Ich möchte etwas erreicht haben, was ich jetzt noch nicht erahnen kann. God women reunited. Happy. Free. Everyone waiting for our next book and discoveries.  21.3.2032: ?

**In five years? How are you going to celebrate?**

Ich bin etabliert als Autorin. Und ich coache. Erfolgreich. Hochpreisig. Bhu Coocu steht und läuft großartig.

21.3.2027: ?

**In three years? How are you going to celebrate?**

21.3.2025
Plötzlich Guru ist ein großer Erfolg für mich und der Vertrag für mein nächstes Buch ist unterschrieben.

**In two years? How are you going to celebrate?**

21.3.2024:
Siehe oben

# GOALS

**In fifty-two weeks? How are you going to celebrate?**

21.3.2023: Plötzlich Buch ist fertig geschrieben, zu meiner vollsten Zufriedenheit und mit von einem großen Verlag veröffentlicht.

**In nine months? How are you going to celebrate?**

Rohentwurf Plötzlich Buch fertig

**In six months? How are you going to celebrate?**

Die ersten 2 Teile sind fertig

**In three months? How are you going to celebrate?**

Ich bin voll im Schreibfluss und Plötzlich Buch schreibt sich wie von selbst

WK 1

# PLANNING

**What are your goals for the upcoming week?**

Schreiner Download Laptop.
Jeden Tag 1 Stunde
Schreiben!
Nächste Szene fertig.

**Have another look. Are you sure this is realistic?
If not, what would be more realistic?**

✓

**What can you do this week to make sure you achieve your goal(s)?**

1 Stunde jeden Tag
Schreiben!

WK 1

# PLANNING

What smaller pieces can you break your goal(s) up into?
Once you're sure you can't break it down anymore, add the sub-goals to the calendar on the next page.

If you don't already have an accountability partner, I strongly suggest you find one or more to help you through the next fifty-two weeks. Who would make a great accountability partner?

*As an alternative, you can always join my group, The Accountable Wordsmiths, on Facebook. The password is CARNELIAN.*

|  | MORNING | AFTERNOON | NIGHT |
|---|---|---|---|
| M: / / | | 15.30 – 17.00 Uhr | |
| T: / / | 6 – 7. | | |
| W: / / | 6 – 7 | | |
| T: / / | 6 – 7 | | |
| F: / / | 6 – 7 | | |
| S: / / | to untold | | |
| S: / / | to untold | | |

# WRITING PROMPT

*Each writing prompt is optional. If, for whatever reason, it does not speak to you, let it be. Who knows? It might make more sense to do the prompt later in the process.*

We all have stories to tell, and there's always at least this one story that we have to tell. That one story that just won't leave us alone, no matter whether we have any inclination to actually write it. Do you know the one? If not, that's all right. Perhaps it will come to you during the exercise. Perhaps it won't; it might not have found you yet.

Grab a notebook or open a new document on your computer and set your timer to fifteen minutes. Now ask the story why it needs to be told. For the next fifteen minutes, write down everything that comes to mind.

You can stop here, but feel free to dig a little deeper. Set your timer to fifteen minutes again and ask the story the following:

What does the story need you for? Why are you the person who needs to write it?

# WEEK 2

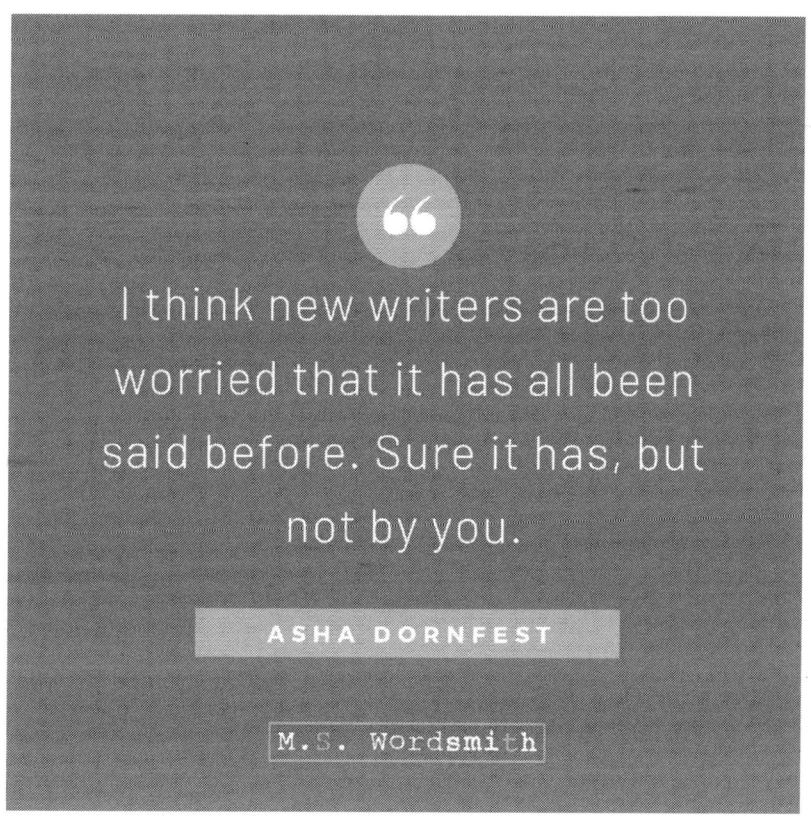

> I think new writers are too worried that it has all been said before. Sure it has, but not by you.
>
> **ASHA DORNFEST**

M.S. Wordsmith

ONE WEEK DOWN, ONLY FIFTY-ONE TO GO.

DATE: _____

# TRACKING

What goal(s) did you set for the past week?

Did you achieve your goal(s)?

# TRACKING

If yes, did you expect too little of yourself, or was your goal just right? If no, what prevented you from achieving it?

If you didn't reach your goals, what can you do next week to make sure you do?

If you picked an accountability partner last week, was this the right person? What worked and what didn't? Is there anything you'll want to do differently next week?

# PLANNING

What are your goals for the upcoming week?

Have another look. Are you sure this is realistic?
If not, what would be more realistic?

What can you do this week to make sure you achieve your goal(s)?

# PLANNING

What smaller pieces can you break your goal(s) up into?
Once you're sure you can't break it down anymore, add the sub-goals to the calendar on the next page.

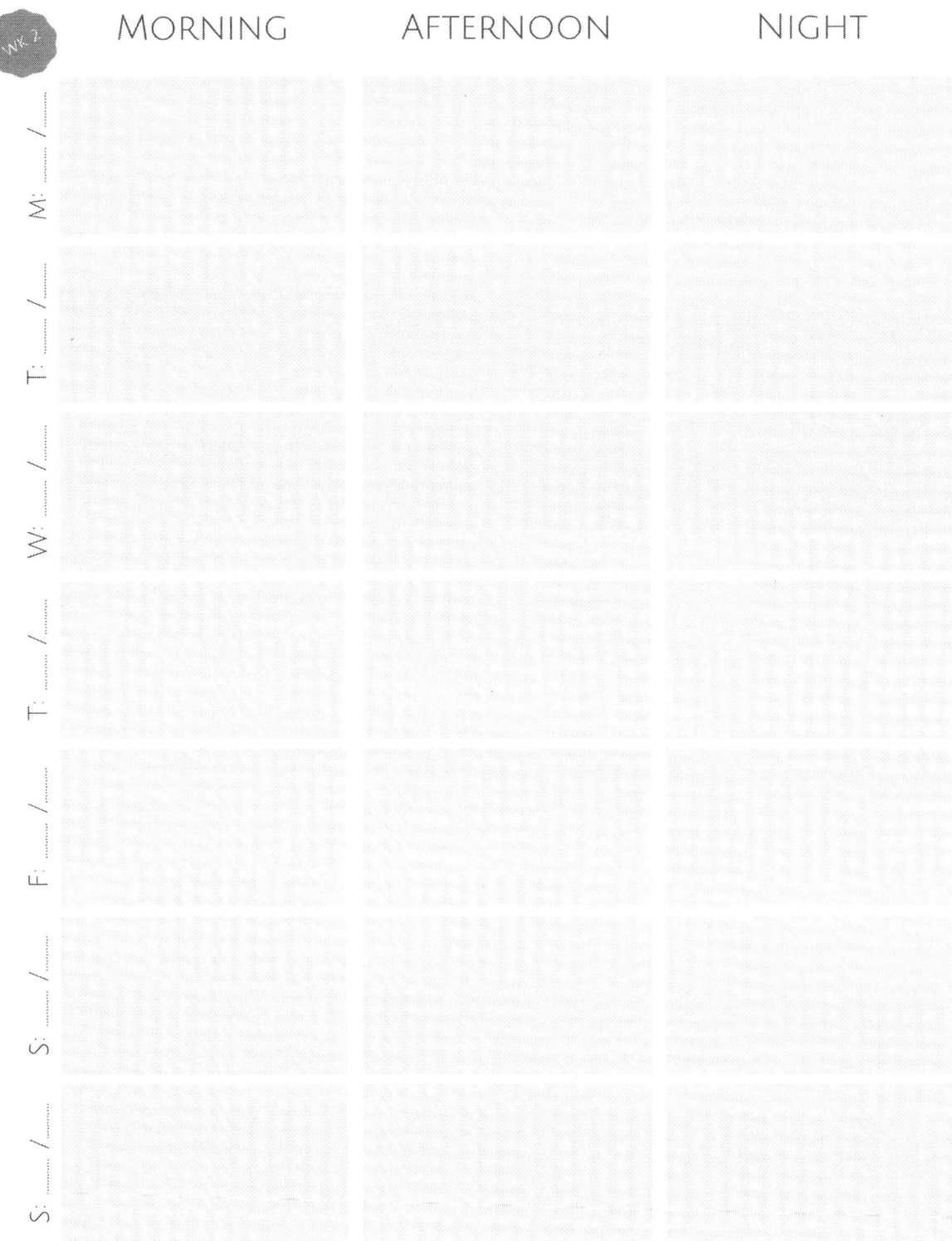

# WRITING PROMPT

*Each writing prompt is optional. If, for whatever reason, it does not speak to you, let it be. Who knows? It might make more sense to do the prompt later in the process.*

Think of a story you are currently working on or want to be working on. In what way is it similar to other stories? In what way is your story different?

Grab a notebook or open a new document on your computer and set your timer to fifteen minutes. For the next quarter of an hour, try to answer the following:

What are you bringing to the table? What voice? Perspective? Knowledge? Angle? What makes your story your story?

# WEEK 3

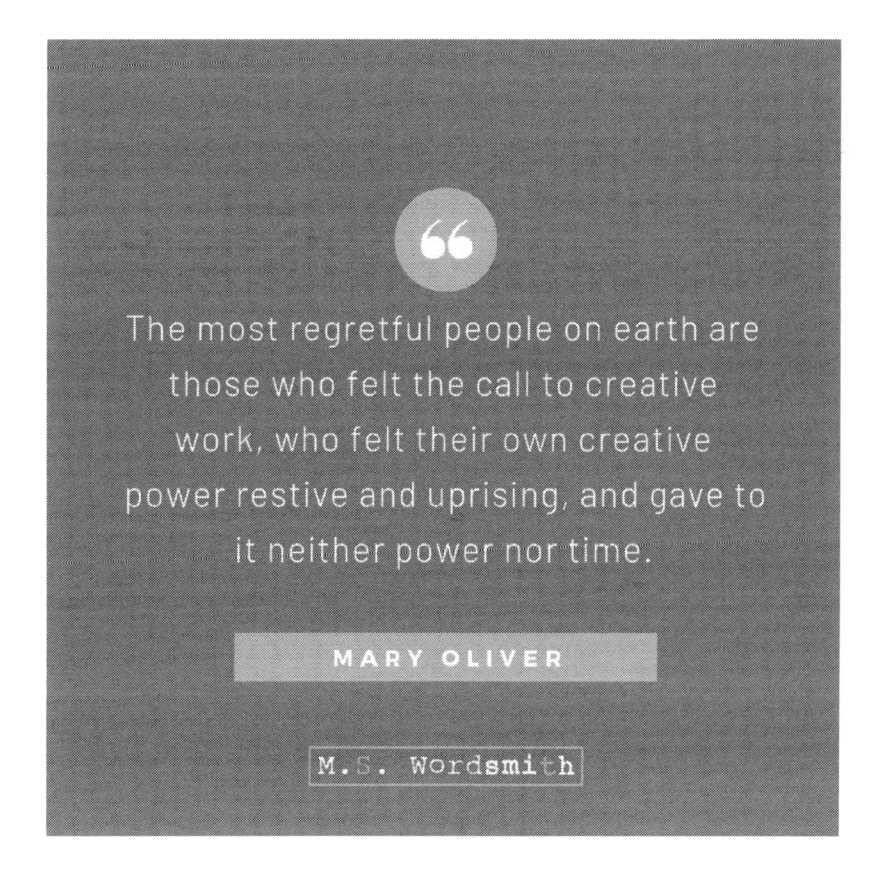

> The most regretful people on earth are those who felt the call to creative work, who felt their own creative power restive and uprising, and gave to it neither power nor time.
>
> **MARY OLIVER**

M.S. Wordsmith

DATE: _____

# Tracking

What goal(s) did you set for the past week?

Did you achieve your goal(s)?

WK 3

# TRACKING

If yes, did you expect too little of yourself, or was your goal just right? If no, what prevented you from achieving it?

If you didn't reach your goals, what can you do next week to make sure you do?

If you picked an accountability partner last week, was this the right person? What worked and what didn't? Is there anything you'll want to do differently next week?

# Planning

What are your goals for the upcoming week?

Have another look. Are you sure this is realistic?
If not, what would be more realistic?

What can you do this week to make sure you achieve your goal(s)?

WK 3

# PLANNING

What smaller pieces can you break your goal(s) up into?
Once you're sure you can't break it down anymore, add the sub-goals to the calendar on the next page.

WK 3

|  | MORNING | AFTERNOON | NIGHT |
|---|---|---|---|
| M: __/__/__ | | | |
| T: __/__/__ | | | |
| W: __/__/__ | | | |
| T: __/__/__ | | | |
| F: __/__/__ | | | |
| S: __/__/__ | | | |
| S: __/__/__ | | | |

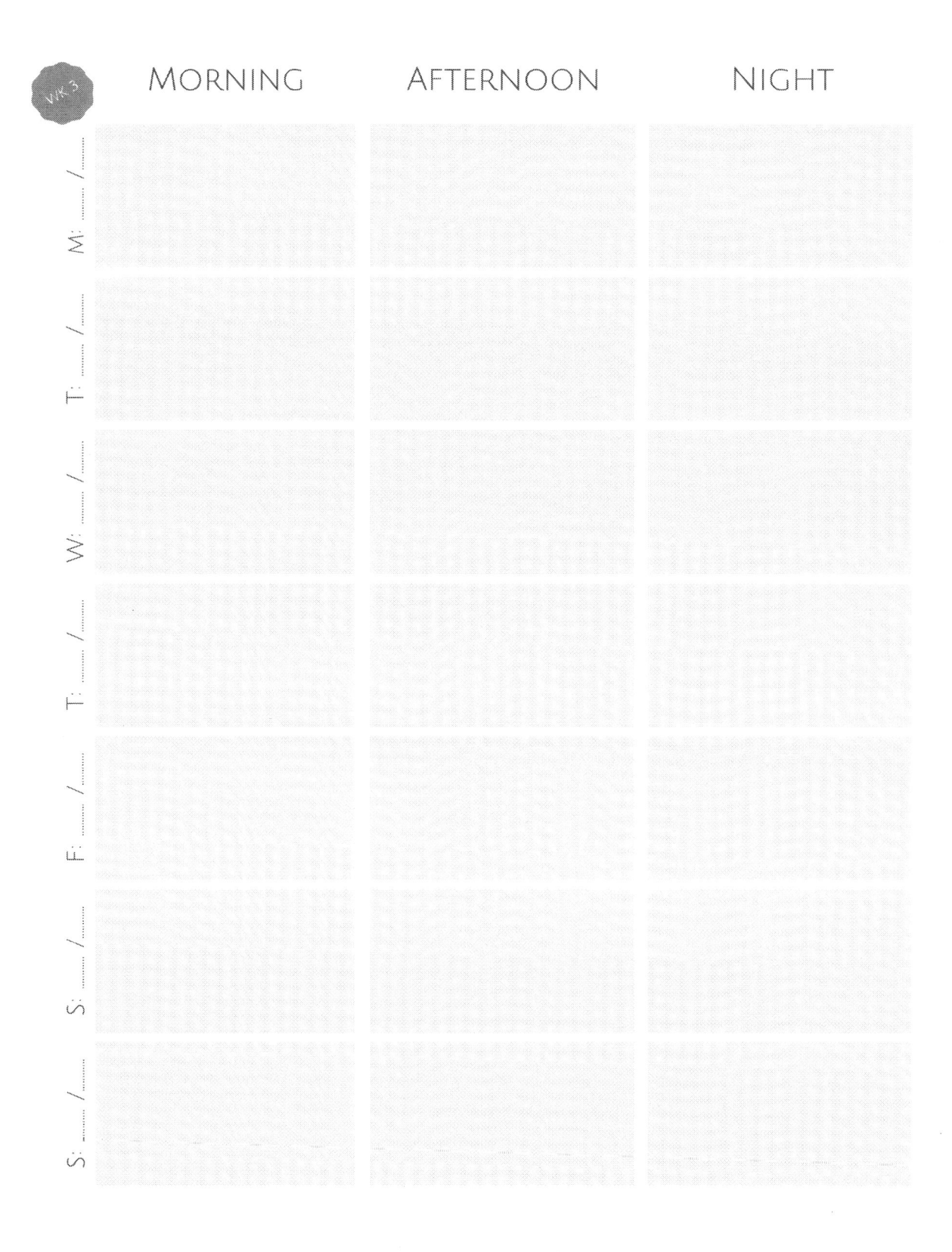

# Writing Prompt

*Each writing prompt is optional. If, for whatever reason, it does not speak to you, let it be. Who knows? It might make more sense to do the prompt later in the process.*

Today is the day you give up on writing. You throw this journal and planner out and decide once and for all: it's not worth your precious time and effort. There's no point in putting pen to paper, or fingers to keyboard; no one wants to hear what you have to say anyway.

Twenty years from now, you haven't written a single word since that day you threw in the towel. Write a letter to the person who gave up, the you living now. Twenty years later, what would you tell yourself about this decision?

# WEEK 4

> **The worst thing you write is better than the best thing you didn't write.**
>
> — AUTHOR UNKNOWN
>
> M.S. Wordsmith

ARE YOU STILL WITH ME?

DATE: ................................................

# Tracking

What goal(s) did you set for the past week?

Did you achieve your goal(s)?

WK 4

# TRACKING

If yes, did you expect too little of yourself, or was your goal just right? If no, what prevented you from achieving it?

If you didn't reach your goals, what can you do next week to make sure you do?

If you picked an accountability partner last week, was this the right person? What worked and what didn't? Is there anything you'll want to do differently next week?

# PLANNING

What are your goals for the upcoming week?

Have another look. Are you sure this is realistic?
If not, what would be more realistic?

What can you do this week to make sure you achieve your goal(s)?

WK 4

# Planning

What smaller pieces can you break your goal(s) up into?
Once you're sure you can't break it down anymore, add the sub-goals to the calendar on the next page.

|  | MORNING | AFTERNOON | NIGHT |
|---|---|---|---|
| M: __/__ | | | |
| T: __/__ | | | |
| W: __/__ | | | |
| T: __/__ | | | |
| F: __/__ | | | |
| S: __/__ | | | |
| S: __/__ | | | |

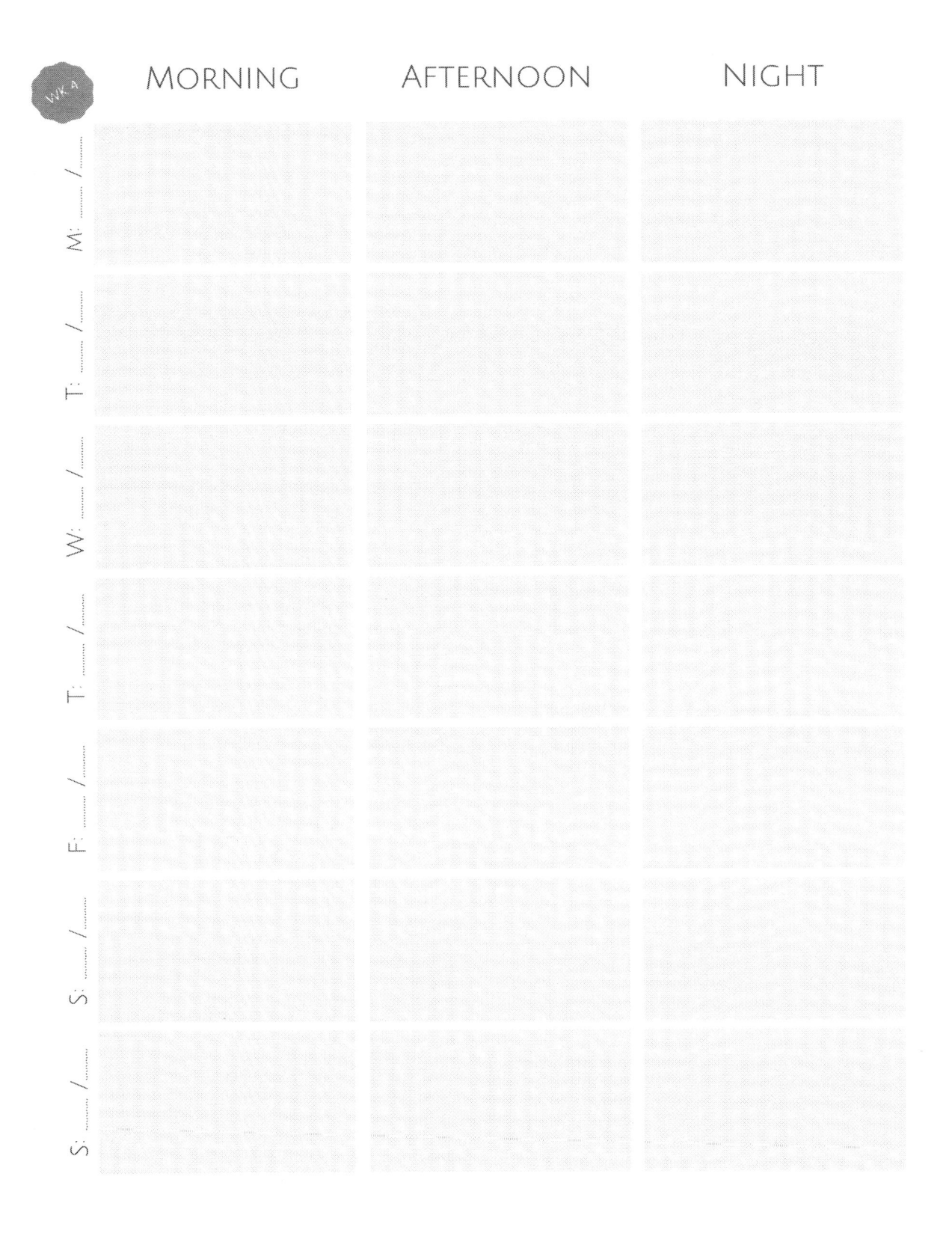

WK 4

# Writing Prompt

*Each writing prompt is optional. If, for whatever reason, it does not speak to you, let it be. Who knows? It might make more sense to do the prompt later in the process.*

Look through some of your previous writing and pick something that you are truly not impressed with. Read it again.

What about it do you like? Consider the details. Is it in the writing? The way you structured the plot? That description you pulled off? Finish the following sentence:

I might not like this story because ............ but I am really pleased with ............, ............, ............, and ............

# WEEK 5

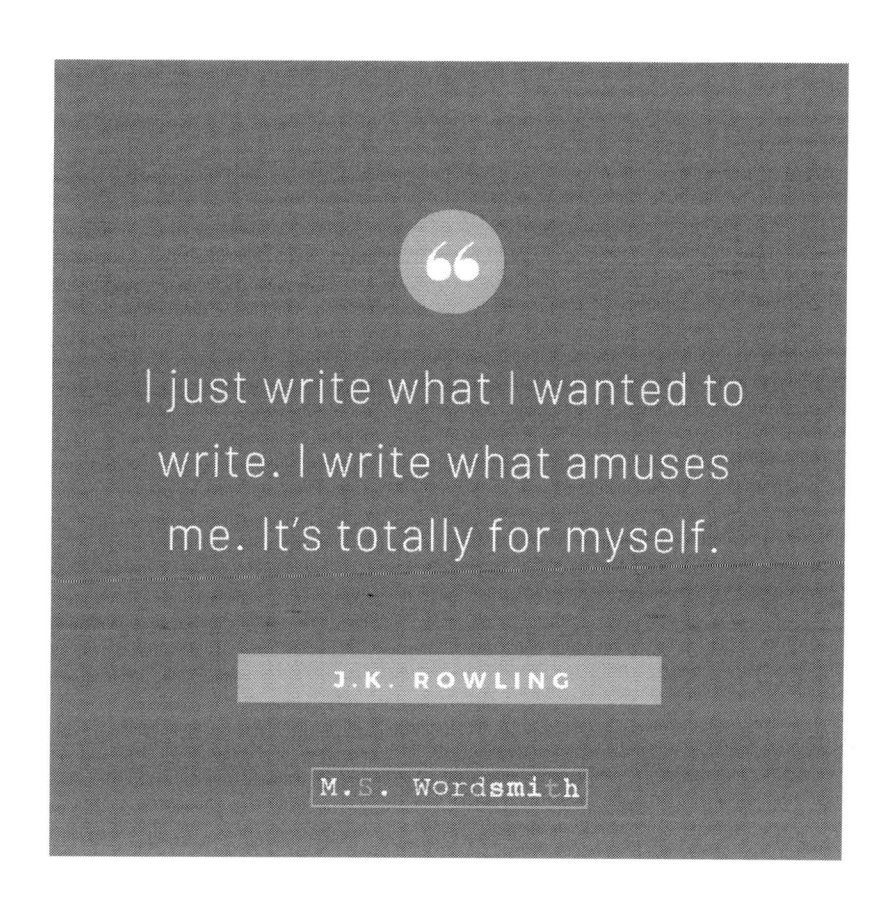

> **❝**
>
> I just write what I wanted to write. I write what amuses me. It's totally for myself.
>
> — J.K. ROWLING

M.S. Wordsmith

DATE: _____

# TRACKING

What goal(s) did you set for the past week?

Did you achieve your goal(s)?

WK 5

# Tracking

If yes, did you expect too little of yourself, or was your goal just right? If no, what prevented you from achieving it?

If you didn't reach your goals, what can you do next week to make sure you do?

If you picked an accountability partner last week, was this the right person? What worked and what didn't? Is there anything you'll want to do differently next week?

# PLANNING

What are your goals for the upcoming week?

Have another look. Are you sure this is realistic?
If not, what would be more realistic?

What can you do this week to make sure you achieve your goal(s)?

WK 5

# Planning

What smaller pieces can you break your goal(s) up into?
Once you're sure you can't break it down anymore, add the sub-goals to the calendar on the next page.

WK 5

wk 5

|  | MORNING | AFTERNOON | NIGHT |
|---|---|---|---|
| M: __ / __ | | | |
| T: __ / __ | | | |
| W: __ / __ | | | |
| T: __ / __ | | | |
| F: __ / __ | | | |
| S: __ / __ | | | |
| S: __ / __ | | | |

# Writing Prompt

*Each writing prompt is optional. If, for whatever reason, it does not speak to you, let it be. Who knows? It might make more sense to do the prompt later in the process.*

Grab a notebook or open a new document on your computer and set your timer to fifteen minutes. For the next quarter of an hour, make a list of all the topics, themes, types of characters, settings, plot twists, and so on that you enjoy as a reader. Don't censor yourself, no one is going to read this if you don't want to.

Once you're done, highlight which of these you've used in your writing. Using another colour, highlight the elements you'd love to write about one day.

# WEEK 6

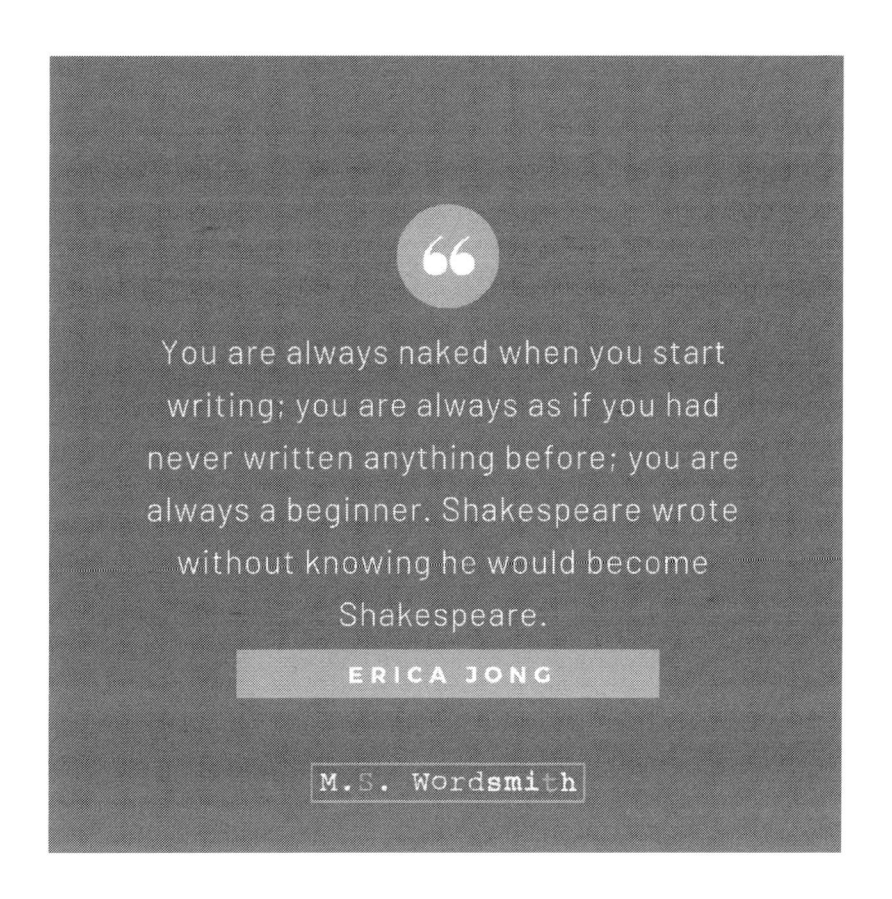

> ❝
>
> You are always naked when you start writing; you are always as if you had never written anything before; you are always a beginner. Shakespeare wrote without knowing he would become Shakespeare.
>
> **ERICA JONG**
>
> M.S. Wordsmith

YOU'VE MADE IT THROUGH THE FIRST FIVE WEEKS, THAT'S MORE THAN A MONTH!

DATE: ........................................................

# Tracking

What goal(s) did you set for the past week?

Did you achieve your goal(s)?

WK 6

# TRACKING

If yes, did you expect too little of yourself, or was your goal just right? If no, what prevented you from achieving it?

If you didn't reach your goals, what can you do next week to make sure you do?

If you picked an accountability partner last week, was this the right person? What worked and what didn't? Is there anything you'll want to do differently next week?

# PLANNING

What are your goals for the upcoming week?

Have another look. Are you sure this is realistic?
If not, what would be more realistic?

What can you do this week to make sure you achieve your goal(s)?

WK 6

# PLANNING

What smaller pieces can you break your goal(s) up into?
Once you're sure you can't break it down anymore, add the sub-goals to the calendar on the next page.

WK 6

WK 6

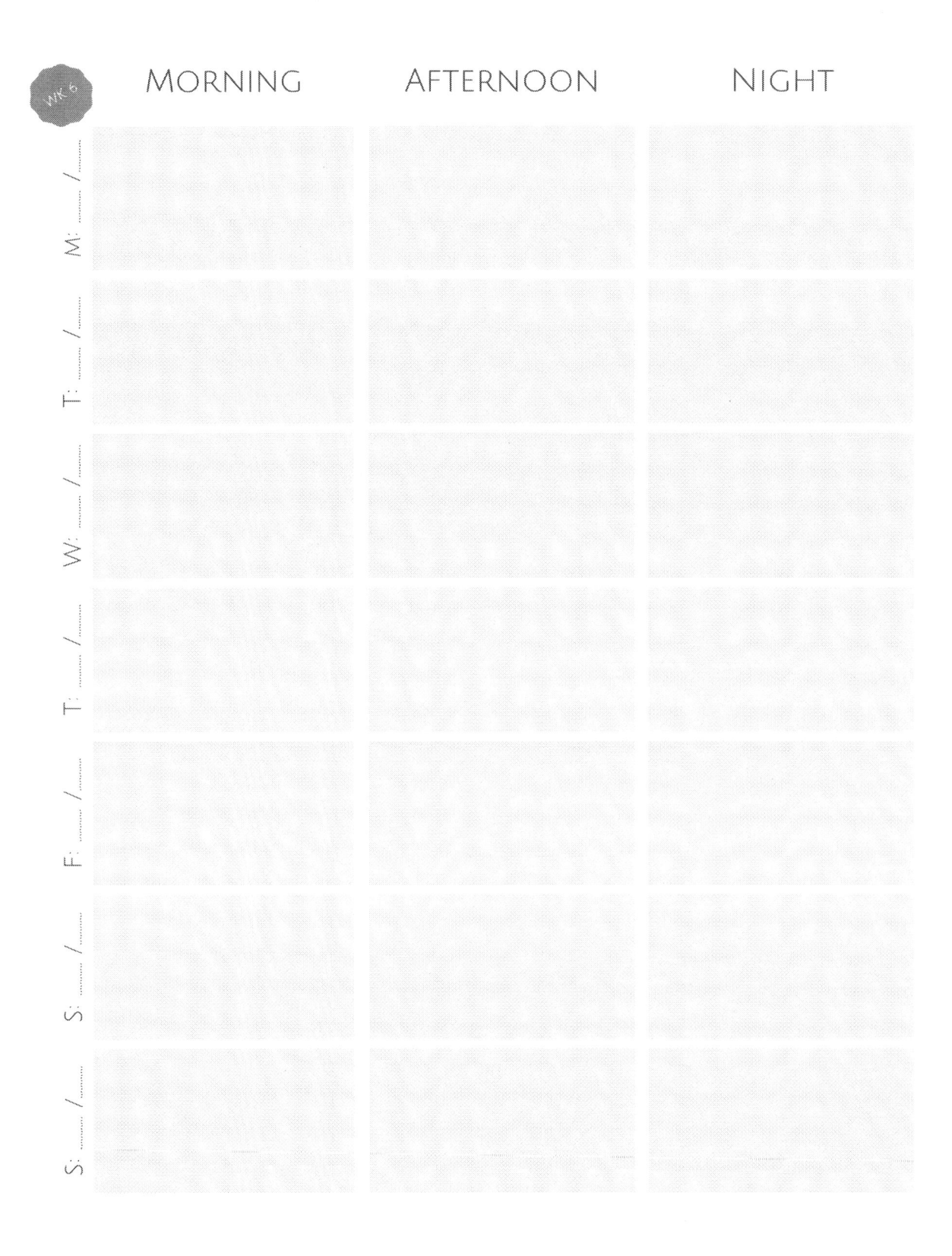

| | MORNING | AFTERNOON | NIGHT |
|---|---|---|---|
| M: / | | | |
| T: / | | | |
| W: / | | | |
| T: / | | | |
| F: / | | | |
| S: / | | | |
| S: / | | | |

# WRITING PROMPT

*Each writing prompt is optional. If, for whatever reason, it does not speak to you, let it be. Who knows? It might make more sense to do the prompt later in the process.*

This week, you'll get to write another letter to the you living now. You can pick from which year you are writing back to your current self. Perhaps you want to write yourself two letters, from different future times?

No matter whether you've become the next J.K. Rowling, Zadie Smith, Stephen King, Angela Carter, Kahlil Gibran, ... , or not, what advice would you give yourself?

# Week 7

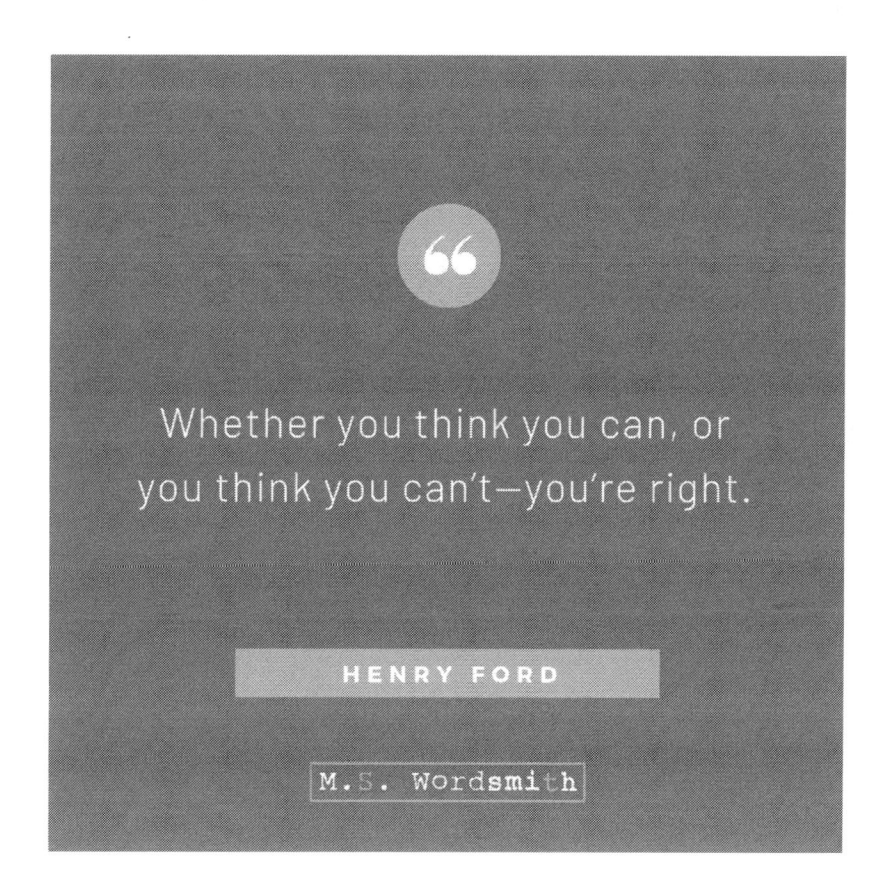

> **"**
>
> Whether you think you can, or you think you can't—you're right.
>
> — HENRY FORD
>
> M.S. Wordsmith

DATE: ...........................................

# Tracking

What goal(s) did you set for the past week?

Did you achieve your goal(s)?

WK 7

# Tracking

If yes, did you expect too little of yourself, or was your goal just right? If no, what prevented you from achieving it?

If you didn't reach your goals, what can you do next week to make sure you do?

If you picked an accountability partner last week, was this the right person? What worked and what didn't? Is there anything you'll want to do differently next week?

# PLANNING

What are your goals for the upcoming week?

Have another look. Are you sure this is realistic?
If not, what would be more realistic?

What can you do this week to make sure you achieve your goal(s)?

# PLANNING

What smaller pieces can you break your goal(s) up into?
Once you're sure you can't break it down anymore, add the sub-goals to the calendar on the next page.

WK 7

|  | Morning | Afternoon | Night |
|---|---|---|---|
| M: / | | | |
| T: / | | | |
| W: / | | | |
| T: / | | | |
| F: / | | | |
| S: / | | | |
| S: / | | | |

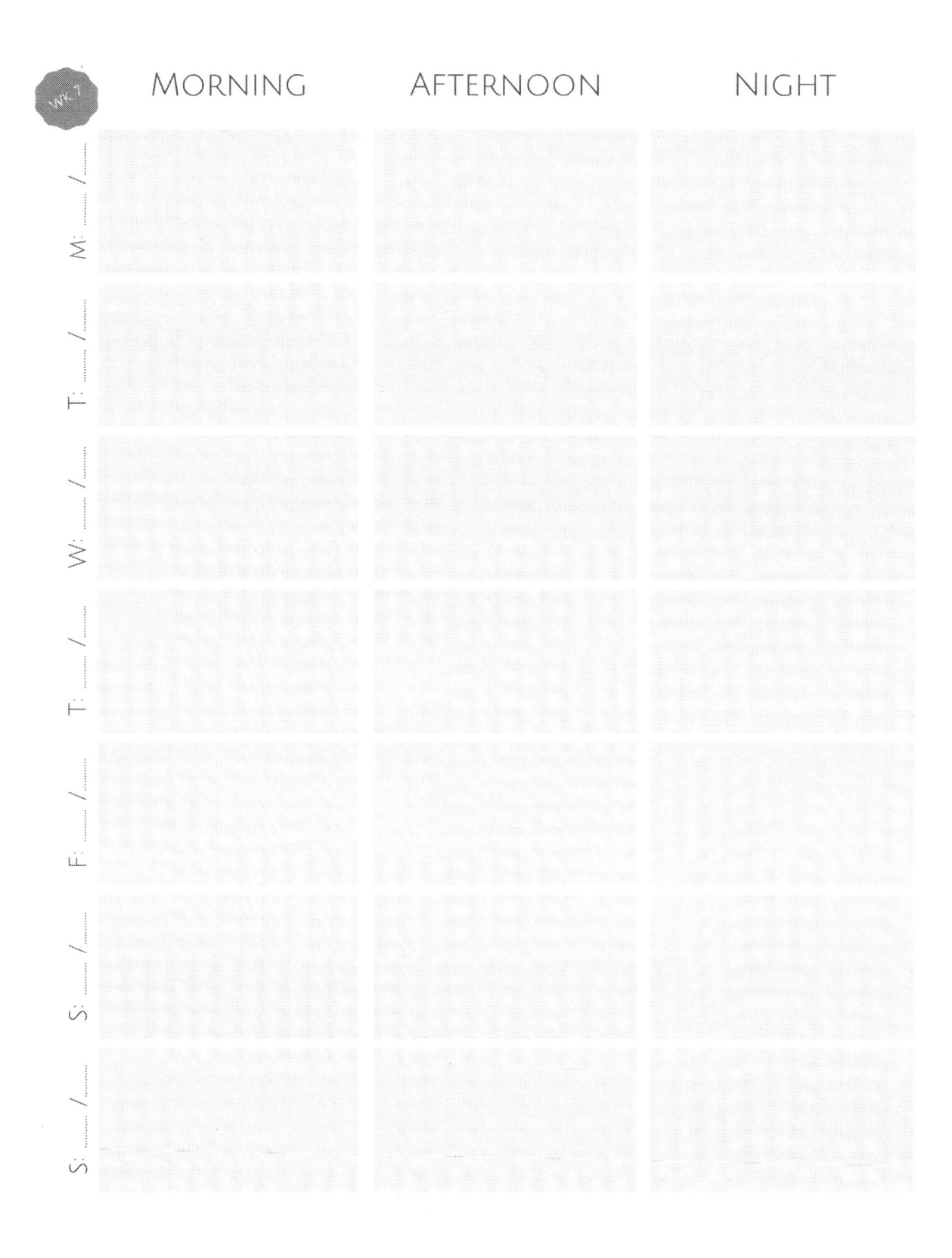

WK 7

# WRITING PROMPT

*Each writing prompt is optional. If, for whatever reason, it does not speak to you, let it be. Who knows? It might make more sense to do the prompt later in the process.*

Grab a notebook or open a new document on your computer. Make a list of all the projects (big and small) you've started in the past but didn't finish. They don't have to be writing related!

When you're done, highlight the ones you didn't finish because you didn't think you could (not the ones you didn't finish because you truly couldn't). Which thoughts kept you from finishing these projects? Do you notice a pattern there or are all of these unrelated issues?

# Week 8

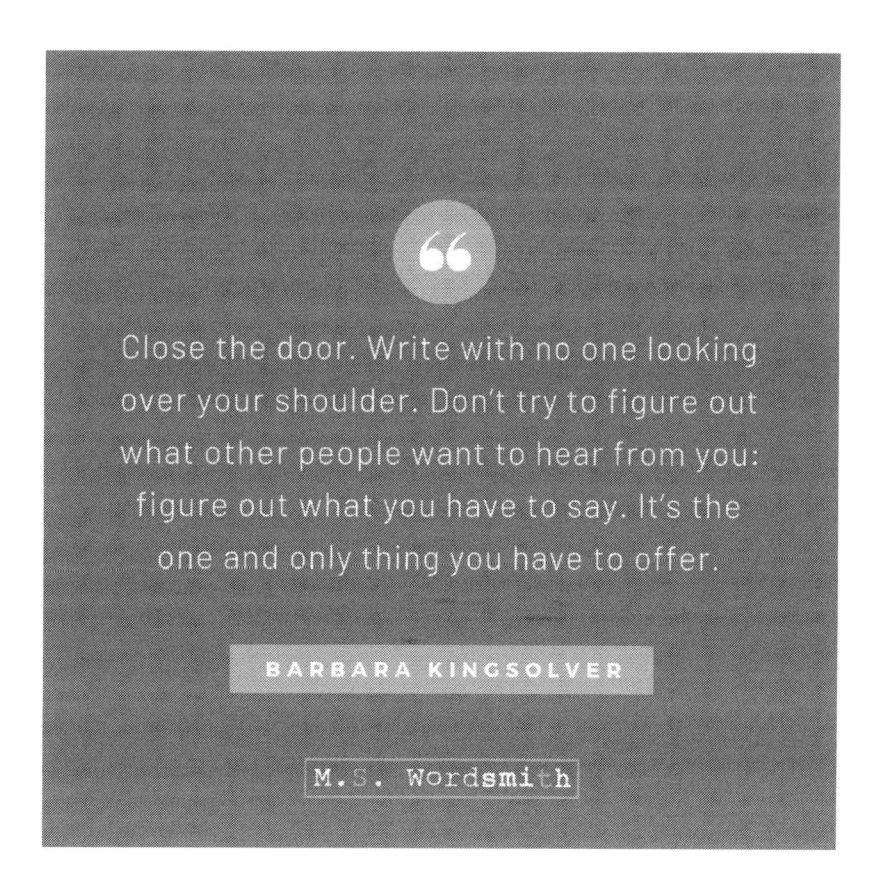

> Close the door. Write with no one looking over your shoulder. Don't try to figure out what other people want to hear from you: figure out what you have to say. It's the one and only thing you have to offer.
>
> **BARBARA KINGSOLVER**
>
> `M.S. Wordsmith`

## Seven weeks done and counting!

DATE: ......................................................

# Tracking

What goal(s) did you set for the past week?

Did you achieve your goal(s)?

WK 8

# TRACKING

If yes, did you expect too little of yourself, or was your goal just right? If no, what prevented you from achieving it?

If you didn't reach your goals, what can you do next week to make sure you do?

If you picked an accountability partner last week, was this the right person? What worked and what didn't? Is there anything you'll want to do differently next week?

WK 8

# PLANNING

What are your goals for the upcoming week?

Have another look. Are you sure this is realistic?
If not, what would be more realistic?

What can you do this week to make sure you achieve your goal(s)?

# PLANNING

What smaller pieces can you break your goal(s) up into?
Once you're sure you can't break it down anymore, add the sub-goals to the calendar on the next page.

|  | MORNING | AFTERNOON | NIGHT |
|---|---|---|---|
| M: __ / __ / __ | | | |
| T: __ / __ / __ | | | |
| W: __ / __ / __ | | | |
| T: __ / __ / __ | | | |
| F: __ / __ / __ | | | |
| S: __ / __ / __ | | | |
| S: __ / __ / __ | | | |

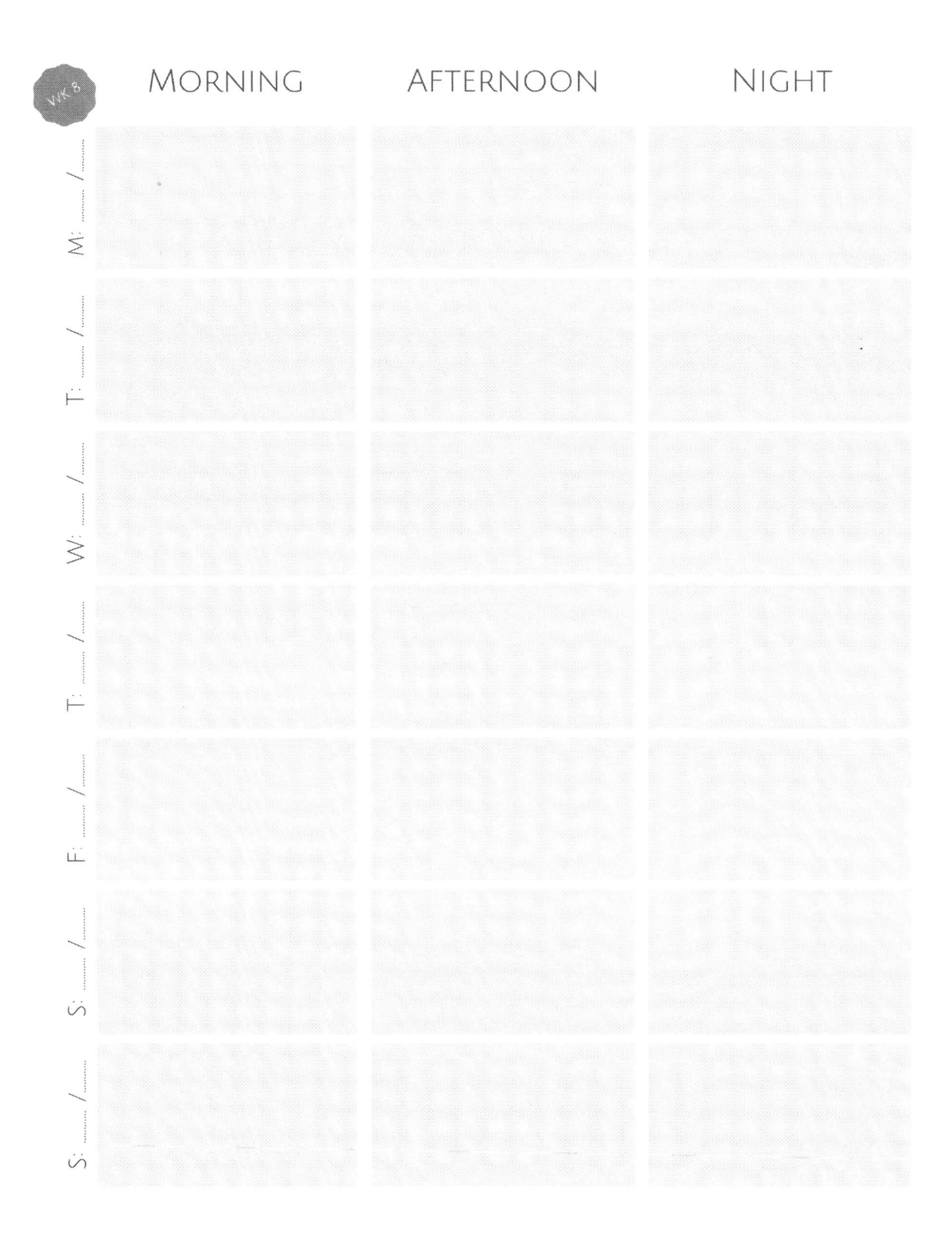

WK 8

# WRITING PROMPT

*Each writing prompt is optional. If, for whatever reason, it does not speak to you, let it be. Who knows? It might make more sense to do the prompt later in the process.*

What would you write if no one was watching?

Grab a notebook or open a new document on your computer. Set the timer and take fifteen minutes to answer this question. Perhaps you end up with a list of topics, a small outline, or a scene.

# WEEK 9

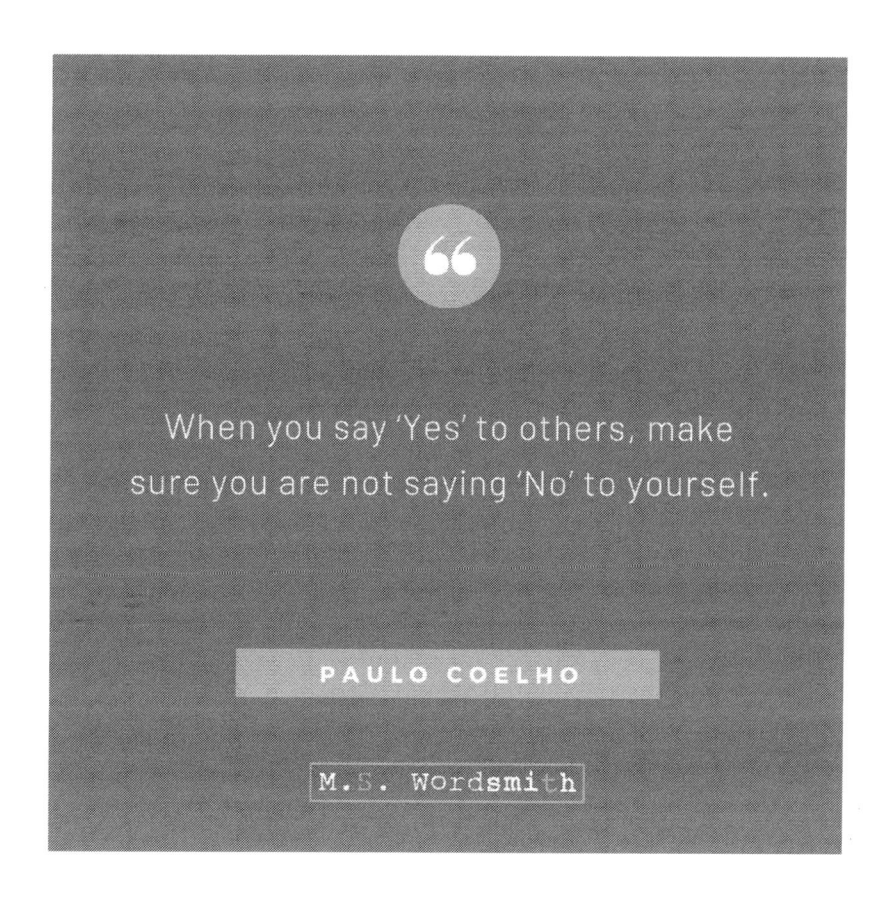

> When you say 'Yes' to others, make sure you are not saying 'No' to yourself.
>
> **PAULO COELHO**
>
> M.S. Wordsmith

DATE: ...........................................................

# Tracking

What goal(s) did you set for the past week?

Did you achieve your goal(s)?

WK 9

# Tracking

If yes, did you expect too little of yourself, or was your goal just right? If no, what prevented you from achieving it?

If you didn't reach your goals, what can you do next week to make sure you do?

If you picked an accountability partner last week, was this the right person? What worked and what didn't? Is there anything you'll want to do differently next week?

# PLANNING

What are your goals for the upcoming week?

Have another look. Are you sure this is realistic?
If not, what would be more realistic?

What can you do this week to make sure you achieve your goal(s)?

WK 9

# PLANNING

What smaller pieces can you break your goal(s) up into?
Once you're sure you can't break it down anymore, add the sub-goals to the calendar on the next page.

WK 9

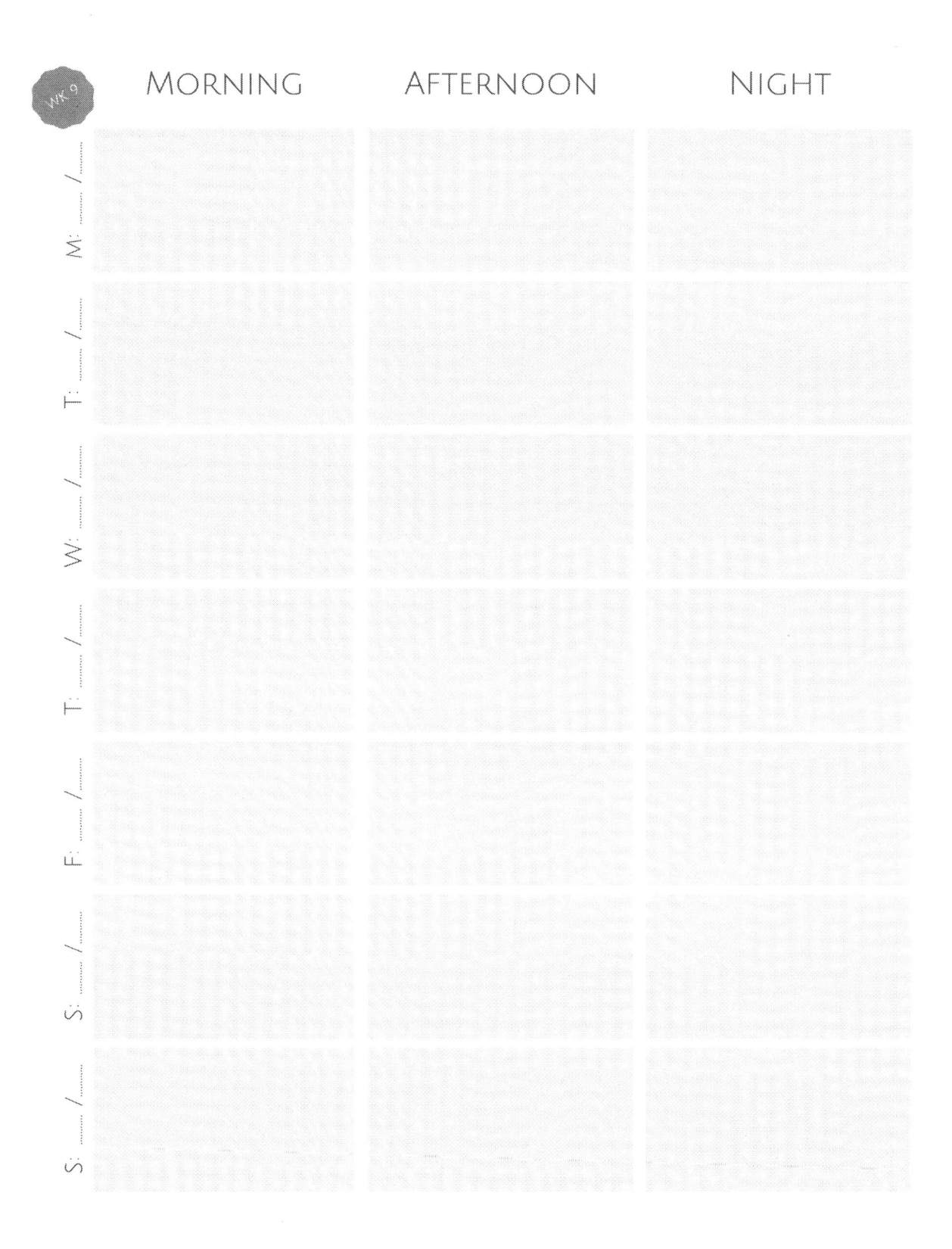

| | MORNING | AFTERNOON | NIGHT |
|---|---|---|---|
| M: __/__ | | | |
| T: __/__ | | | |
| W: __/__ | | | |
| T: __/__ | | | |
| F: __/__ | | | |
| S: __/__ | | | |
| S: __/__ | | | |

# Writing Prompt

*Each writing prompt is optional. If, for whatever reason, it does not speak to you, let it be. Who knows? It might make more sense to do the prompt later in the process.*

Do you struggle saying 'Yes' to yourself? If so, is that only when it comes to your writing, or is this an issue in multiple areas of your life? Grab a notebook or open a new document on your computer. Set the timer to ten minutes and make a list of all the things that fill your cup.

If you want to dig a little deeper, set the timer again and – for each item on your list – write down how often you would need these to occur for your cup to be filled. On a weekly basis, once a month, every quarter?

Feel free to take the next step as well: for every item on your list, what is it you need (to do) to be able to say 'Yes' to yourself?

# WEEK 10

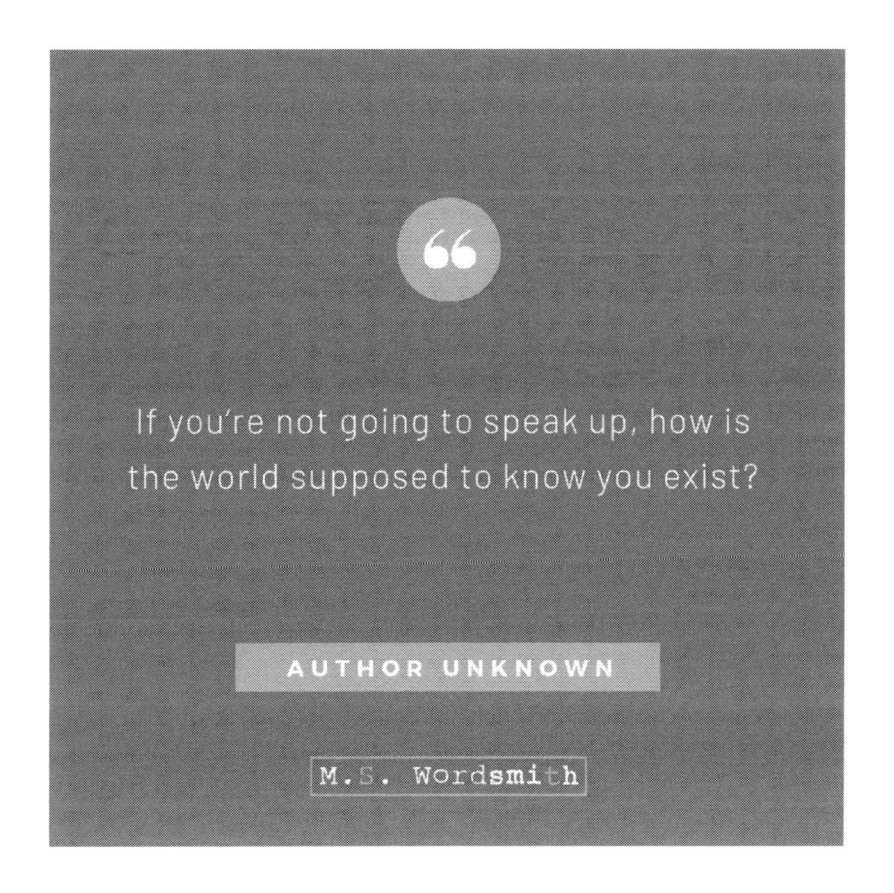

> If you're not going to speak up, how is the world supposed to know you exist?

**AUTHOR UNKNOWN**

M.S. Wordsmith

ARE YOU COMFORTABLE SHARING YOUR WORK WITH THE WORLD? IF SO, YOU'LL ENJOY THIS WEEK'S WRITING PROMPT.

DATE: ..................................................

# TRACKING

What goal(s) did you set for the past week?

Did you achieve your goal(s)?

WK 10

# Tracking

If yes, did you expect too little of yourself, or was your goal just right? If no, what prevented you from achieving it?

If you didn't reach your goals, what can you do next week to make sure you do?

If you picked an accountability partner last week, was this the right person? What worked and what didn't? Is there anything you'll want to do differently next week?

# PLANNING

What are your goals for the upcoming week?

Have another look. Are you sure this is realistic?
If not, what would be more realistic?

What can you do this week to make sure you achieve your goal(s)?

WK 10

# Planning

What smaller pieces can you break your goal(s) up into?
Once you're sure you can't break it down anymore, add the sub-goals to the calendar on the next page.

|  | MORNING | AFTERNOON | NIGHT |
|---|---|---|---|
| WK 10 | | | |
| M: __ / __ | | | |
| T: __ / __ | | | |
| W: __ / __ | | | |
| T: __ / __ | | | |
| F: __ / __ | | | |
| S: __ / __ | | | |
| S: __ / __ | | | |

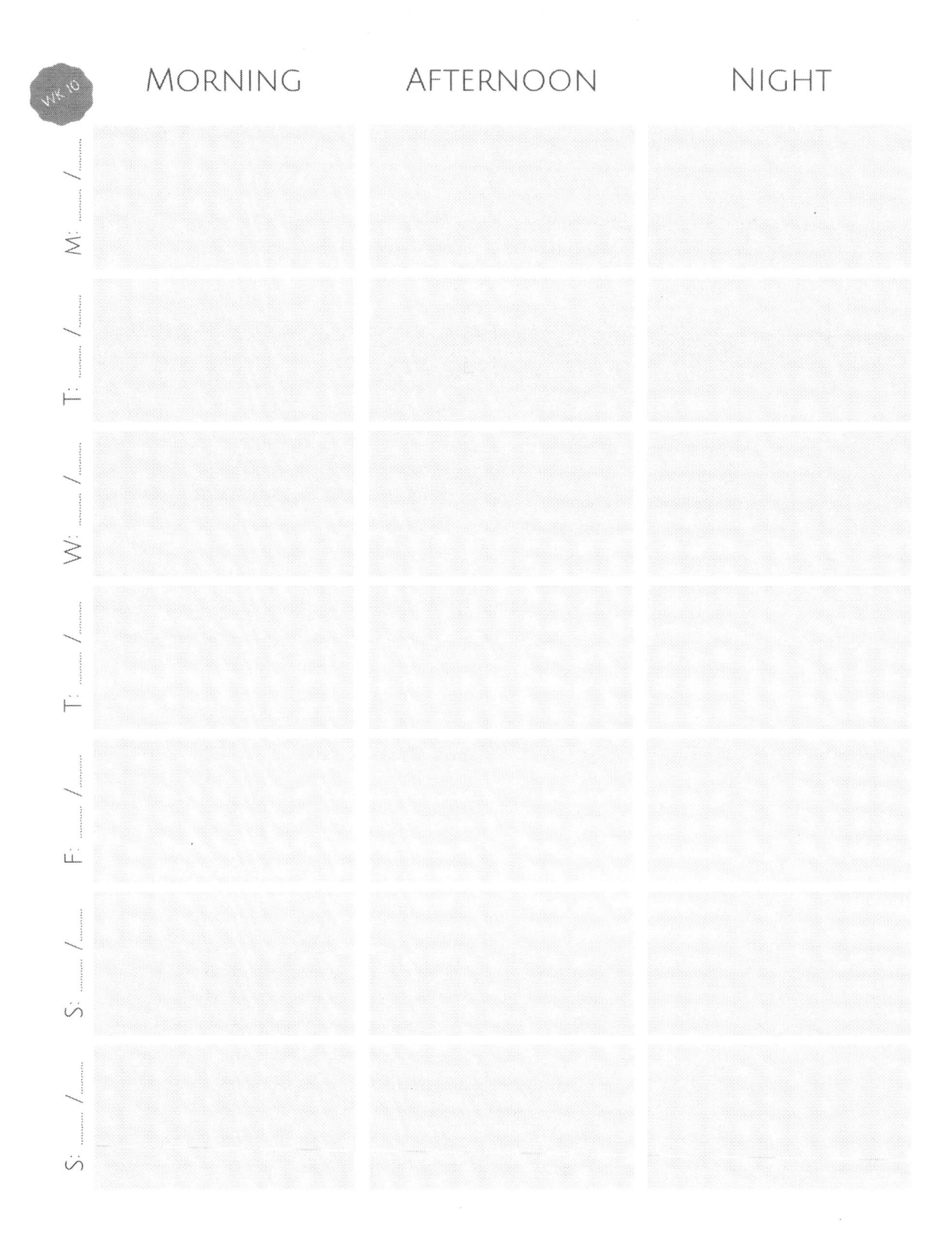

# Writing Prompt

*Each writing prompt is optional. If, for whatever reason, it does not speak to you, let it be. Who knows? It might make more sense to do the prompt later in the process.*

Look through some of your writing and pick something that you're quite happy with. A bit of dialogue, a poem, a scene. It doesn't have to be perfect. Take ten minutes to see if it needs to be altered in any way.

Now open one of your social media channels and post it. I'm not kidding. Feel free to explain why you're posting it, but do post it.

If you're not a social media person, send it to a friend or a group of friends via email or snail mail. No excuses!

# WEEK 11

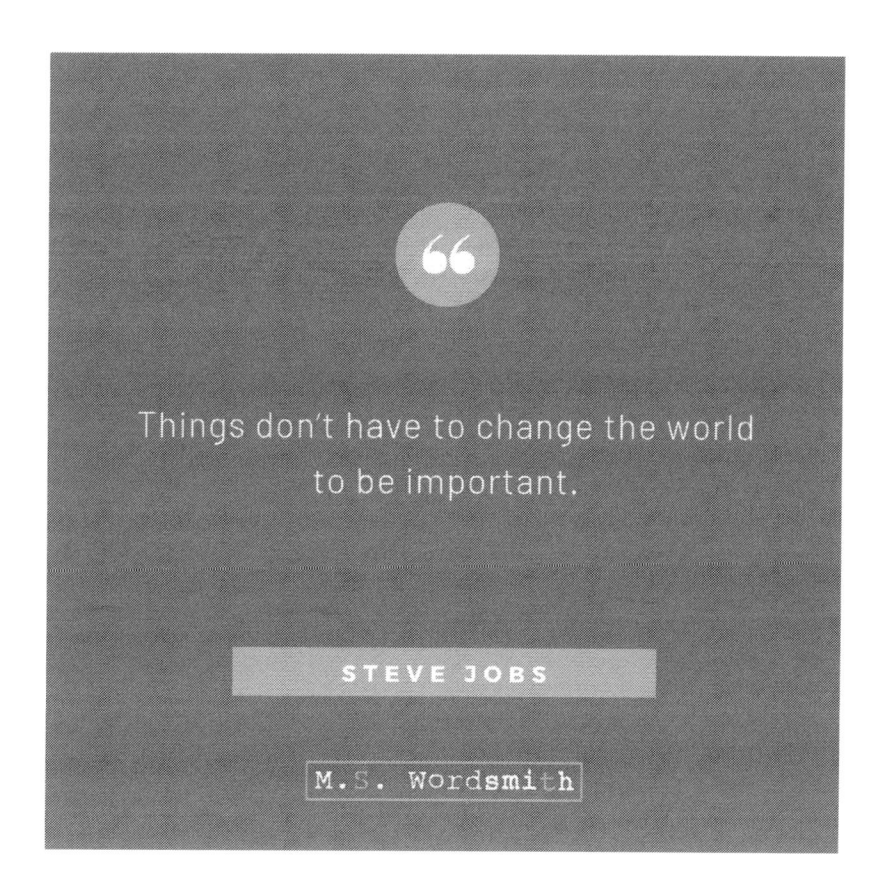

> Things don't have to change the world to be important.
>
> **STEVE JOBS**
>
> M.S. Wordsmith

DATE: ..................................................

# TRACKING

What goal(s) did you set for the past week?

Did you achieve your goal(s)?

WK 11

# TRACKING

If yes, did you expect too little of yourself, or was your goal just right? If no, what prevented you from achieving it?

If you didn't reach your goals, what can you do next week to make sure you do?

If you picked an accountability partner last week, was this the right person? What worked and what didn't? Is there anything you'll want to do differently next week?

# PLANNING

What are your goals for the upcoming week?

Have another look. Are you sure this is realistic?
If not, what would be more realistic?

What can you do this week to make sure you achieve your goal(s)?

WK 11

# Planning

What smaller pieces can you break your goal(s) up into?
Once you're sure you can't break it down anymore, add the sub-goals to the calendar on the next page.

WK 11

| | MORNING | AFTERNOON | NIGHT |
|---|---|---|---|
| M: __/__ | | | |
| T: __/__ | | | |
| W: __/__ | | | |
| T: __/__ | | | |
| F: __/__ | | | |
| S: __/__ | | | |
| S: __/__ | | | |

# Writing Prompt

*Each writing prompt is optional. If, for whatever reason, it does not speak to you, let it be. Who knows? It might make more sense to do the prompt later in the process.*

Why are your stories important to you? Grab a notebook or open a new document on your laptop. Set the timer and take fifteen minutes to answer this question.

Can you imagine other people finding your stories important for exactly those reasons?

# Week 12

> **The scariest moment is always just before you start.**
>
> — STEPHEN KING
>
> M.S. Wordsmith

ELEVEN WEEKS HAVE COME AND GONE! DID THAT TIME FLY BY FOR YOU OR NOT AT ALL?

DATE: _____

# TRACKING

What goal(s) did you set for the past week?

Did you achieve your goal(s)?

WK 12

# Tracking

If yes, did you expect too little of yourself, or was your goal just right? If no, what prevented you from achieving it?

If you didn't reach your goals, what can you do next week to make sure you do?

If you picked an accountability partner last week, was this the right person? What worked and what didn't? Is there anything you'll want to do differently next week?

# PLANNING

What are your goals for the upcoming week?

Have another look. Are you sure this is realistic?
If not, what would be more realistic?

What can you do this week to make sure you achieve your goal(s)?

# Planning

What smaller pieces can you break your goal(s) up into?
Once you're sure you can't break it down anymore, add the sub-goals to the calendar on the next page.

WK 12

**WK 12**

| | Morning | Afternoon | Night |
|---|---|---|---|
| M: / | | | |
| T: / | | | |
| W: / | | | |
| T: / | | | |
| F: / | | | |
| S: / | | | |
| S: / | | | |

# WRITING PROMPT

*Each writing prompt is optional. If, for whatever reason, it does not speak to you, let it be. Who knows? It might make more sense to do the prompt later in the process.*

Each time you put pen to paper, or start typing away on your keyboard, you're conquering the white page. You're doing the work. For a moment, forget about the times you didn't get the words down and take a moment to celebrate all the times you did. Can you remember what it felt like to conquer that blank page?

Grab a notebook or open a new document on your computer to write down exactly how it made you feel. Each time the fear hits you again and you're about to tell yourself you can't do it, return to this moment and remember. You can do it. You're just scared. There's nothing wrong with that. Just don't let it keep you from doing what you want to do.

# Week 13

> The function of the first draft is to help you figure out your story. The function of every draft after that is to figure out the most dramatic way to tell that story.
>
> **DARCY PATTISON**

M.S. Wordsmith

DATE: _____

# TRACKING

What goal(s) did you set for the past week?

Did you achieve your goal(s)?

WK 13

# TRACKING

If yes, did you expect too little of yourself, or was your goal just right? If no, what prevented you from achieving it?

If you didn't reach your goals, what can you do next week to make sure you do?

If you picked an accountability partner last week, was this the right person? What worked and what didn't? Is there anything you'll want to do differently next week?

# PLANNING

What are your goals for the upcoming week?

Have another look. Are you sure this is realistic?
If not, what would be more realistic?

What can you do this week to make sure you achieve your goal(s)?

# Planning

What smaller pieces can you break your goal(s) up into?
Once you're sure you can't break it down anymore, add the sub-goals to the calendar on the next page.

WK 13

| | MORNING | AFTERNOON | NIGHT |
|---|---|---|---|
| M: __ / __ | | | |
| T: __ / __ | | | |
| W: __ / __ | | | |
| T: __ / __ | | | |
| F: __ / __ | | | |
| S: __ / __ | | | |
| S: __ / __ | | | |

# Writing Prompt

*Each writing prompt is optional. If, for whatever reason, it does not speak to you, let it be. Who knows? It might make more sense to do the prompt later in the process.*

Are you able to turn off your internal editor while writing a first draft or do you keep going back as you write? Wanting to get it right the first time is one of the biggest motivation killers. It's like Ernest Hemingway once said:

'The first draft of anything is shit.'

This week, I dare you to write without once looking back. Just focus on the finish line. There's plenty of time to edit your work, once you've reached the end. You won't know what you have until you've gotten it all down.

YOU'VE MADE IT THROUGH THE FIRST THREE MONTHS!

# How are you going to celebrate?

Write it down, then go do it!

# Week 14

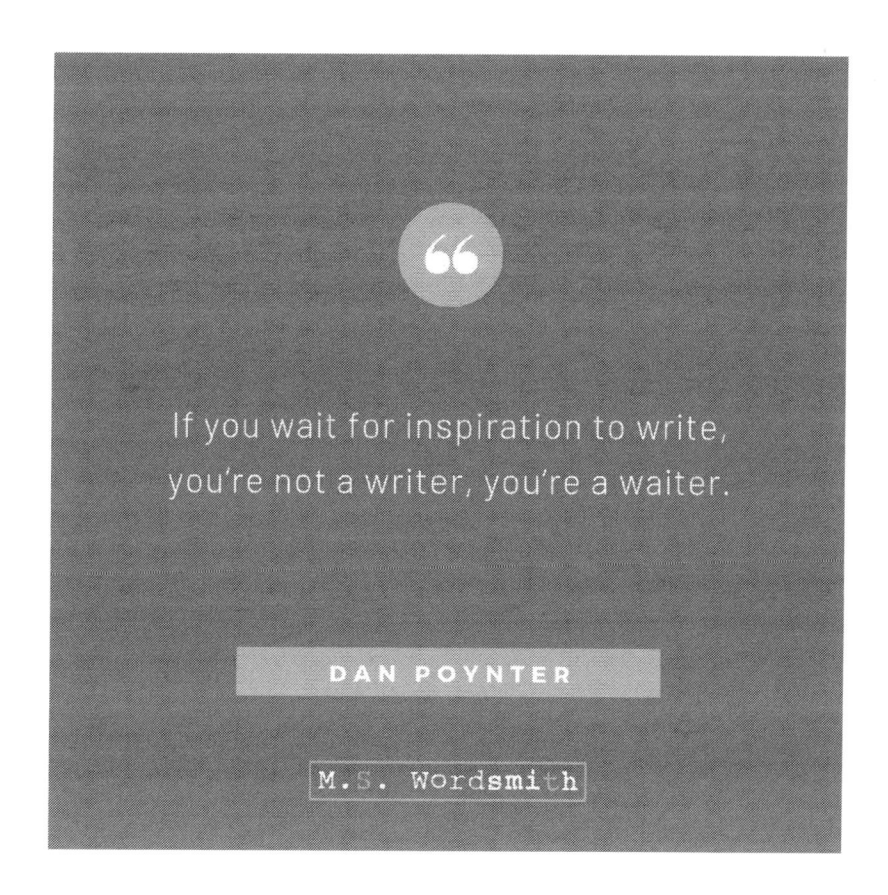

> If you wait for inspiration to write, you're not a writer, you're a waiter.
>
> **DAN POYNTER**
>
> M.S. Wordsmith

DATE: ........................................

# CLARITY

During Week One, you wrote down why you were first called to write. Over the past three months, have you been able to reconnect to that calling? Take a moment to reflect.

Over the past three months, have you been able to reconnect to how writing used to make you feel? There are no right or wrong answers here. Like the calling, your feelings about writing might have shifted. Take a moment to reflect on this as well.

# CLARITY

Looking back over the past three months, how did the act of writing make you feel? How did you feel right before you started, during, and once you were done?

Are you dealing with the same struggles and roadblocks you identified when we started this journey, or have they changed? If they have, what are you currently struggling with?

# CLARITY

For each struggle and roadblock you are (still) dealing with, can you determine which are internal or external? Even if your list hasn't changed, still reflect on this. Something might very well have shifted in the meantime.

# CLARITY

For each struggle and roadblock, what do you think you need to overcome it? If you're still dealing with the same struggle(s) or roadblock(s), this doesn't mean you didn't make any progress. This is where you get to determine whether you did.

# REFLECTING

Let's take a moment to reflect. When looking back on the past three months, what are you most grateful for?

What are the most significant lessons you have learned about yourself and your writing?

Did you achieve your 3-month goal(s)? If yes, (how) did you celebrate? If not, what steps could you take from this week onwards to ensure you reach your next 3-month goal(s)?

# GOALS

*Do these goals still hold true or is it time to adjust them?*

Where do you want to be in the next fifty-two weeks? How are you going to celebrate?

In nine months? How are you going to celebrate?

In six months? How are you going to celebrate?

In three months? How are you going to celebrate?

# Tracking

What goal(s) did you set for the past week?

Did you achieve your goal(s)?

WK 14

# Tracking

If yes, did you expect too little of yourself, or was your goal just right? If no, what prevented you from achieving it?

If you didn't reach your goals, what can you do next week to make sure you do?

If you picked an accountability partner last week, was this the right person? What worked and what didn't? Is there anything you'll want to do differently next week?

WK 14

# PLANNING

What are your goals for the upcoming week?

Have another look. Are you sure this is realistic?
If not, what would be more realistic?

What can you do this week to make sure you achieve your goal(s)?

WK 14

# PLANNING

What smaller pieces can you break your goal(s) up into?
Once you're sure you can't break it down anymore, add the sub-goals to the calendar on the next page.

WK 14

WK 14

| | MORNING | AFTERNOON | NIGHT |
|---|---|---|---|
| M: / / | | | |
| T: / / | | | |
| W: / / | | | |
| T: / / | | | |
| F: / / | | | |
| S: / / | | | |
| S: / / | | | |

# WRITING PROMPT

*Each writing prompt is optional. If, for whatever reason, it does not speak to you, let it be. Who knows? It might make more sense to do the prompt later in the process.*

Is it easy for you to sit down in that chair and make yourself write?

This week, try to write at a different location each day. If you usually write at the kitchen table, move to the living room. If you tend to write from home, try that new coffee place with the free Wi-Fi, or check out the library. Each day, reflect on your writing.

Was it easier to get the words down? Harder? Did you go faster than usual, or slower? Did you feel more or less inspired?

# Week 15

> "
>
> Write like it matters, and it will.
>
> **LIBBA BRAY**

M.S. Wordsmith

DATE: _____

# Tracking

What goal(s) did you set for the past week?

Did you achieve your goal(s)?

WK 15

# Tracking

If yes, did you expect too little of yourself, or was your goal just right? If no, what prevented you from achieving it?

If you didn't reach your goals, what can you do next week to make sure you do?

If you picked an accountability partner last week, was this the right person? What worked and what didn't? Is there anything you'll want to do differently next week?

# Planning

What are your goals for the upcoming week?

Have another look. Are you sure this is realistic?
If not, what would be more realistic?

What can you do this week to make sure you achieve your goal(s)?

WK 15

# PLANNING

What smaller pieces can you break your goal(s) up into?
Once you're sure you can't break it down anymore, add the sub-goals to the calendar on the next page.

WK 15

| | Morning | Afternoon | Night |
|---|---|---|---|
| WK 15 | | | |
| M: __/__ | | | |
| T: __/__ | | | |
| W: __/__ | | | |
| T: __/__ | | | |
| F: __/__ | | | |
| S: __/__ | | | |
| S: __/__ | | | |

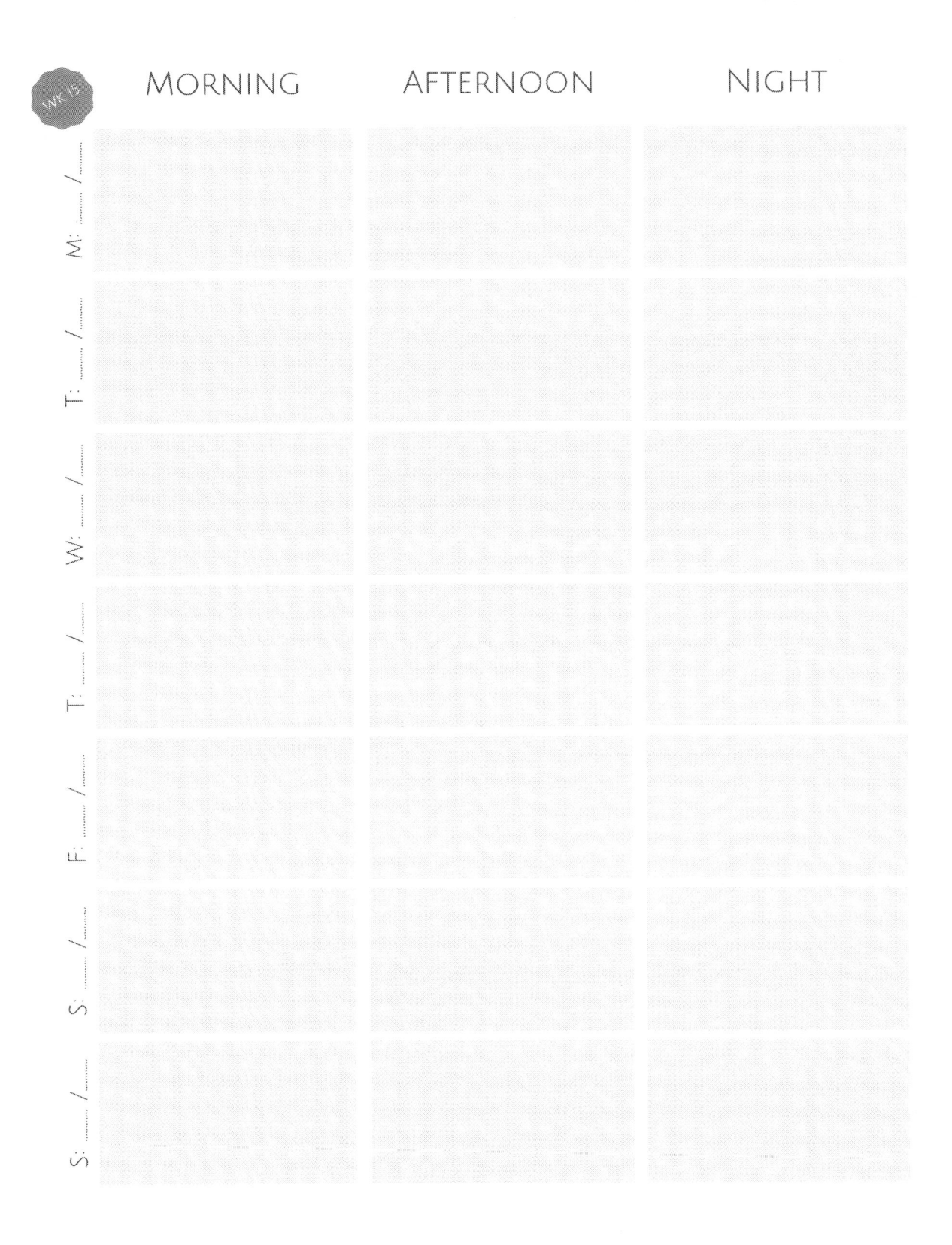

# WRITING PROMPT

*Each writing prompt is optional. If, for whatever reason, it does not speak to you, let it be. Who knows? It might make more sense to do the prompt later in the process.*

Has any of your writing ever made you laugh? Angry? Cry? Smile? Select a piece of writing this week and let someone read it. Look at their faces when they are reading it: are they going through the same motions as you did when you wrote it?

# WEEK 16

> What is the best way to write? Each of us has to discover her own way by writing. Writing teaches writing. No one can tell you your own secret.
>
> **GAIL SHER**

M.S. Wordsmith

HERE WE ARE, 105 DAYS IN. THEY SAY IT TAKES ABOUT 100 DAYS TO CREATE A HABIT. SO THAT BEGS THE QUESTION: DOES WRITING FEEL LIKE A HABIT YET?

DATE: ........................................................

# Tracking

What goal(s) did you set for the past week?

Did you achieve your goal(s)?

WK 16

# Tracking

If yes, did you expect too little of yourself, or was your goal just right? If no, what prevented you from achieving it?

If you didn't reach your goals, what can you do next week to make sure you do?

If you picked an accountability partner last week, was this the right person? What worked and what didn't? Is there anything you'll want to do differently next week?

# PLANNING

What are your goals for the upcoming week?

Have another look. Are you sure this is realistic?
If not, what would be more realistic?

What can you do this week to make sure you achieve your goal(s)?

# Planning

What smaller pieces can you break your goal(s) up into?
Once you're sure you can't break it down anymore, add the sub-goals to the calendar on the next page.

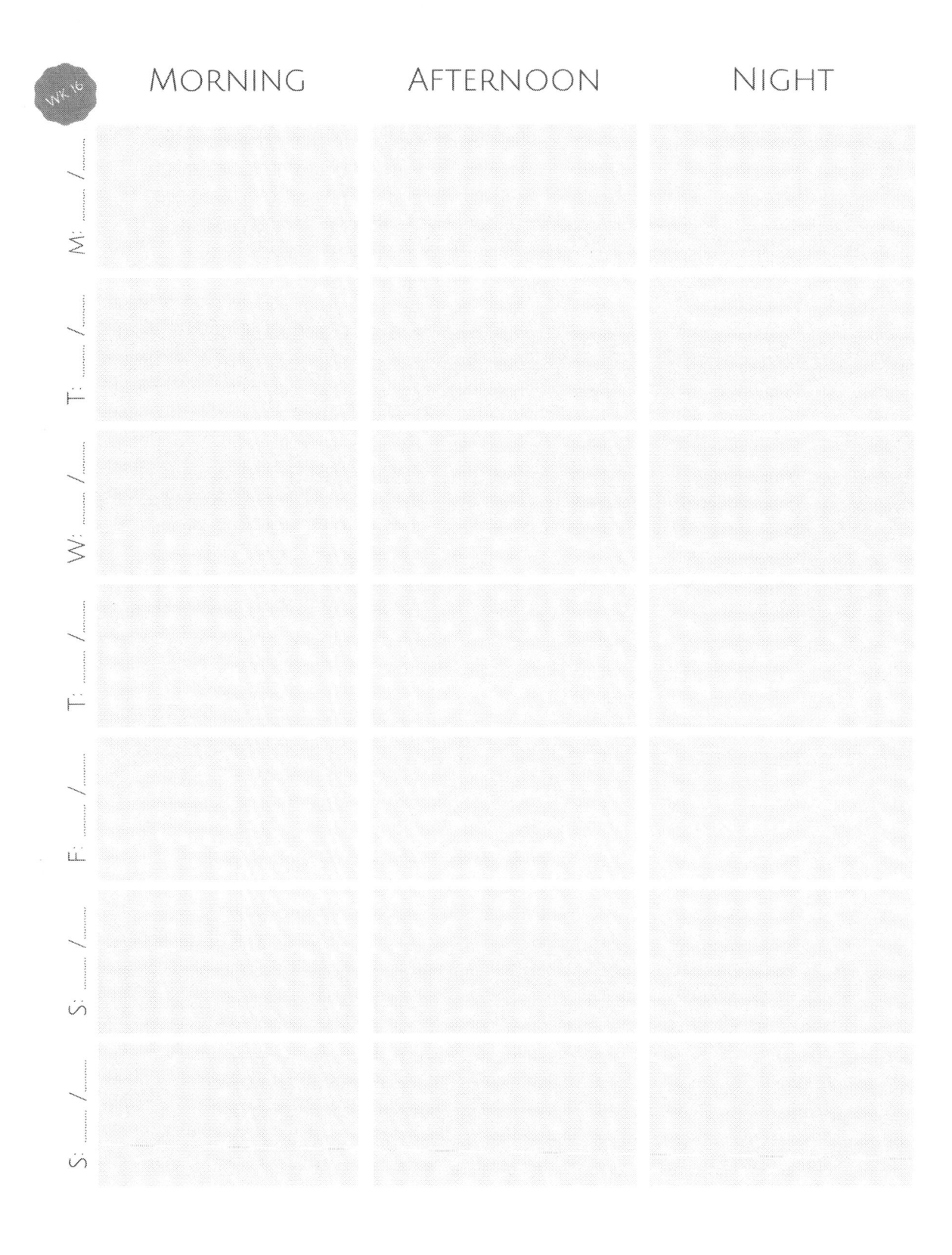

## WK. 16

|  | Morning | Afternoon | Night |
|---|---|---|---|
| M: __/__ | | | |
| T: __/__ | | | |
| W: __/__ | | | |
| T: __/__ | | | |
| F: __/__ | | | |
| S: __/__ | | | |
| S: __/__ | | | |

# Writing prompt

*Each writing prompt is optional. If, for whatever reason, it does not speak to you, let it be. Who knows? It might make more sense to do the prompt later in the process.*

No matter how many books are out there, suggesting this or that writing method or habit, there are as many ways of writing as there are writers. However, this doesn't mean you have to figure out your own best way from scratch.

This week, look into different writing habits and methods. Go online and look at what other writers did or are doing. Does any of it resonate? Be eclectic and test whatever speaks to you; don't feel like you need to adopt their entire system. Just pick the bits that work for you and move on, leaving behind the parts that don't feel right.

# Week 17

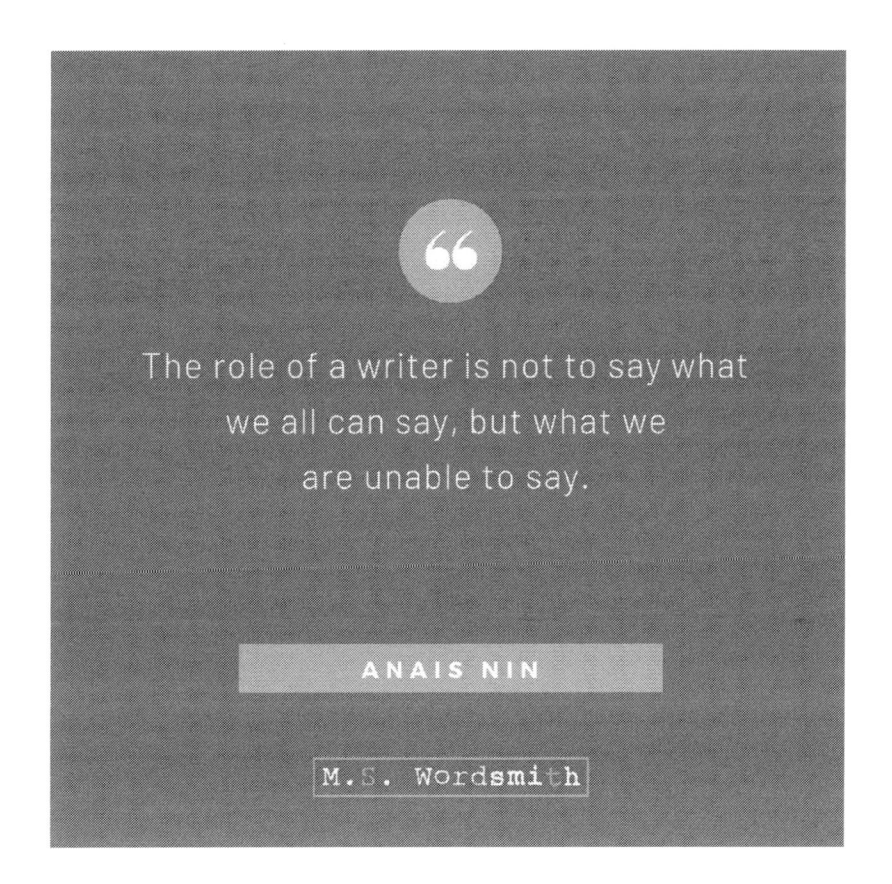

> The role of a writer is not to say what we all can say, but what we are unable to say.
>
> **ANAIS NIN**
>
> M.S. Wordsmith

DATE: ...........................................................

# Tracking

What goal(s) did you set for the past week?

Did you achieve your goal(s)?

# Tracking

If yes, did you expect too little of yourself, or was your goal just right? If no, what prevented you from achieving it?

If you didn't reach your goals, what can you do next week to make sure you do?

If you picked an accountability partner last week, was this the right person? What worked and what didn't? Is there anything you'll want to do differently next week?

# PLANNING

What are your goals for the upcoming week?

Have another look. Are you sure this is realistic?
If not, what would be more realistic?

What can you do this week to make sure you achieve your goal(s)?

WK 17

# PLANNING

What smaller pieces can you break your goal(s) up into?
Once you're sure you can't break it down anymore, add the sub-goals to the calendar on the next page.

| | Morning | Afternoon | Night |
|---|---|---|---|
| M: __/__ | | | |
| T: __/__ | | | |
| W: __/__ | | | |
| T: __/__ | | | |
| F: __/__ | | | |
| S: __/__ | | | |
| S: __/__ | | | |

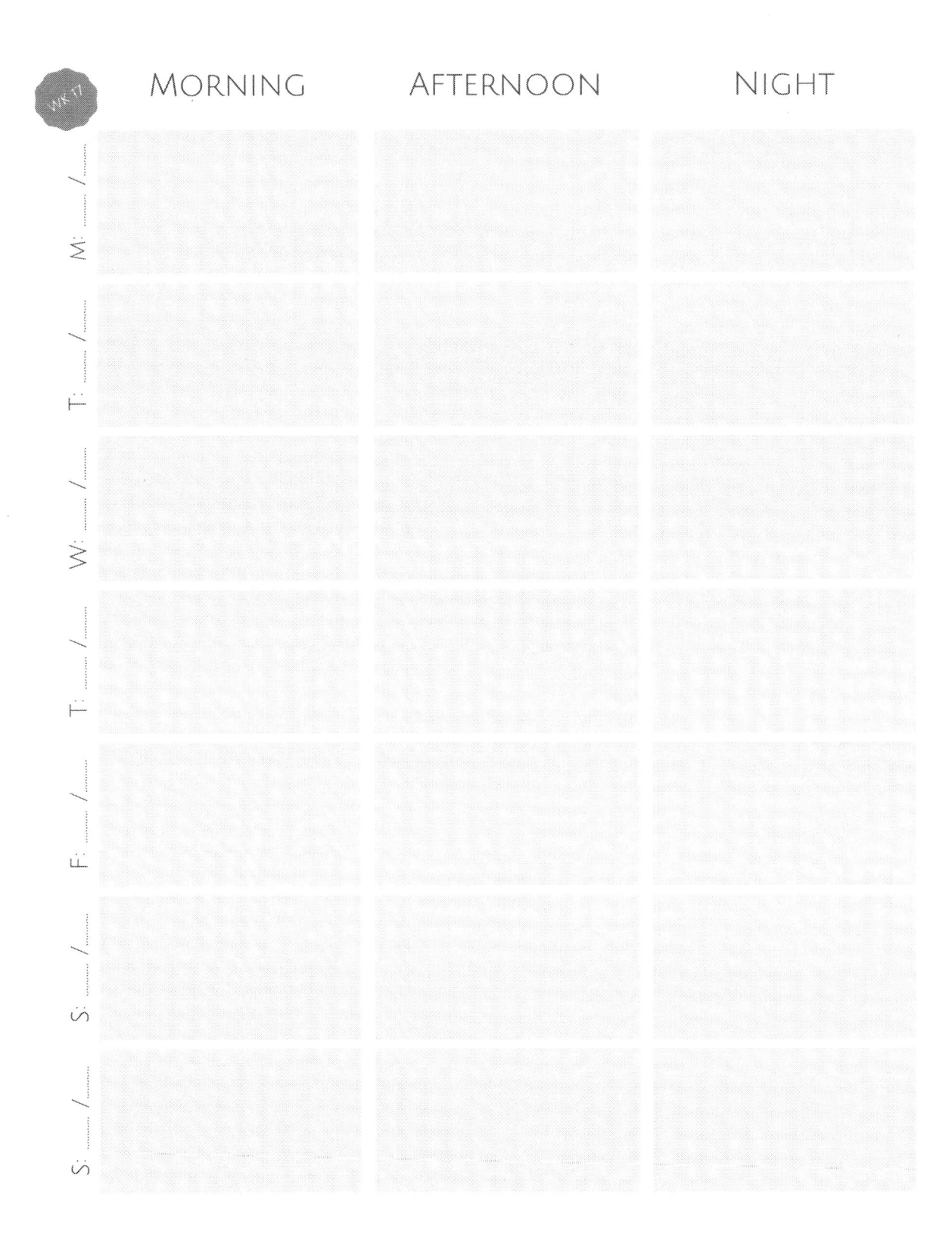

WK 17

# WRITING PROMPT

*Each writing prompt is optional. If, for whatever reason, it does not speak to you, let it be. Who knows? It might make more sense to do the prompt later in the process.*

Grab a notebook or open a new document on your computer. Set the timer to twenty minutes and write down what only you can say, the story only you can tell.

If you want to dig a little deeper after completing this exercise, go back to Week One and compare notes. Does anything in particular strike you?

# WEEK 18

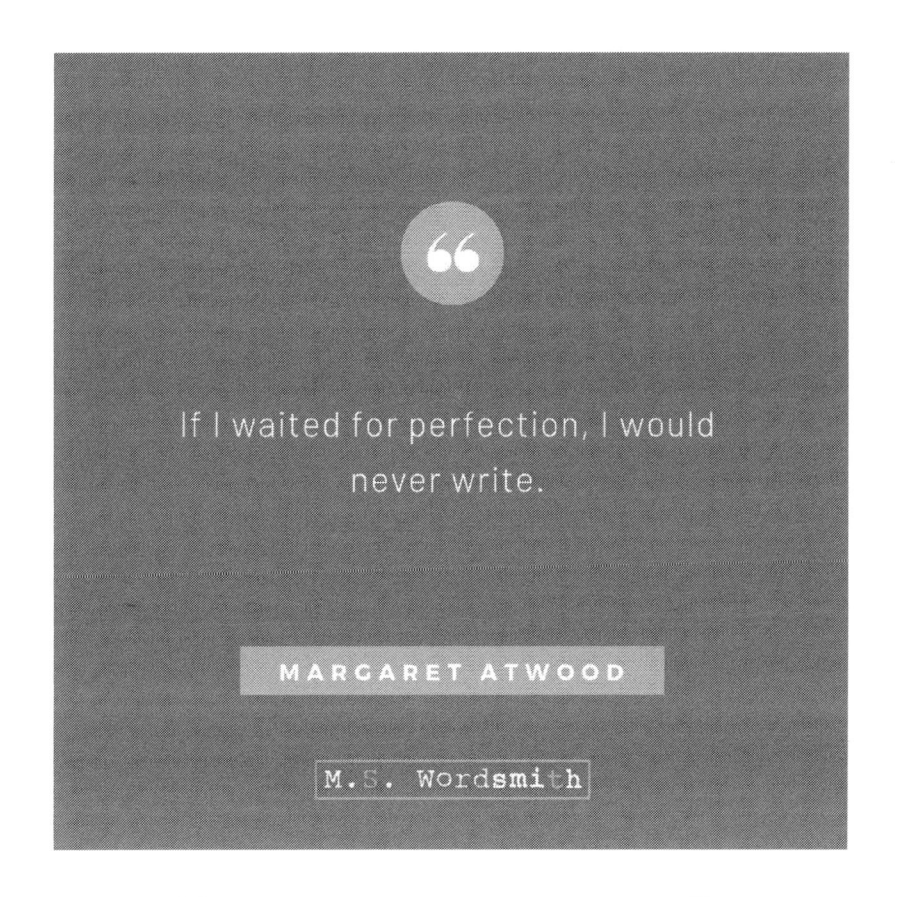

> "If I waited for perfection, I would never write.
>
> **MARGARET ATWOOD**
>
> M.S. Wordsmith

HOW ARE YOU HOLDING UP?
STILL GOING STRONG?

DATE: ...........................................................

# Tracking

What goal(s) did you set for the past week?

Did you achieve your goal(s)?

WK 18

# TRACKING

If yes, did you expect too little of yourself, or was your goal just right? If no, what prevented you from achieving it?

If you didn't reach your goals, what can you do next week to make sure you do?

If you picked an accountability partner last week, was this the right person? What worked and what didn't? Is there anything you'll want to do differently next week?

# PLANNING

What are your goals for the upcoming week?

Have another look. Are you sure this is realistic?
If not, what would be more realistic?

What can you do this week to make sure you achieve your goal(s)?

# PLANNING

What smaller pieces can you break your goal(s) up into?
Once you're sure you can't break it down anymore, add the sub-goals to the calendar on the next page.

WK 18

|  | MORNING | AFTERNOON | NIGHT |
|---|---|---|---|
| M: / | | | |
| T: / | | | |
| W: / | | | |
| T: / | | | |
| F: / | | | |
| S: / | | | |
| S: / | | | |

# WRITING PROMPT

*Each writing prompt is optional. If, for whatever reason, it does not speak to you, let it be. Who knows? It might make more sense to do the prompt later in the process.*

Think of a book or other piece of writing that you truly enjoyed. Was it perfect? Would you have changed a thing if you could have? (If not, let me know the title, OK? I need to see this for myself!) In all seriousness, no finished piece is every truly finished, and different readers will find different 'mistakes'.

This week, share a first draft of something you wrote and ask for positive feedback only. That's right, only positive!

Don't forget to reflect on the exercise.

# WEEK 19

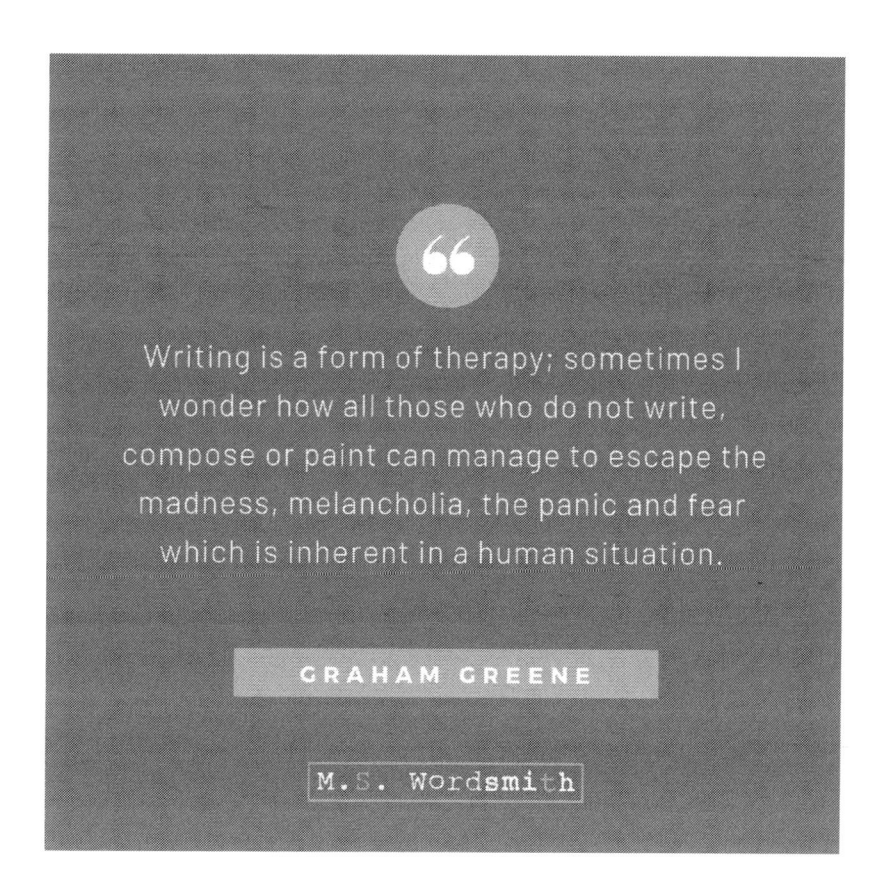

> Writing is a form of therapy; sometimes I wonder how all those who do not write, compose or paint can manage to escape the madness, melancholia, the panic and fear which is inherent in a human situation.
>
> **GRAHAM GREENE**

M.S. Wordsmith

DATE: ...........................................................

# Tracking

What goal(s) did you set for the past week?

Did you achieve your goal(s)?

WK 19

# Tracking

If yes, did you expect too little of yourself, or was your goal just right? If no, what prevented you from achieving it?

If you didn't reach your goals, what can you do next week to make sure you do?

If you picked an accountability partner last week, was this the right person? What worked and what didn't? Is there anything you'll want to do differently next week?

# PLANNING

What are your goals for the upcoming week?

Have another look. Are you sure this is realistic?
If not, what would be more realistic?

What can you do this week to make sure you achieve your goal(s)?

# PLANNING

What smaller pieces can you break your goal(s) up into?
Once you're sure you can't break it down anymore, add the sub-goals to the calendar on the next page.

WK 19

|  | Morning | Afternoon | Night |
|---|---|---|---|
| WK 19 | | | |
| M: __/__ | | | |
| T: __/__ | | | |
| W: __/__ | | | |
| T: __/__ | | | |
| F: __/__ | | | |
| S: __/__ | | | |
| S: __/__ | | | |

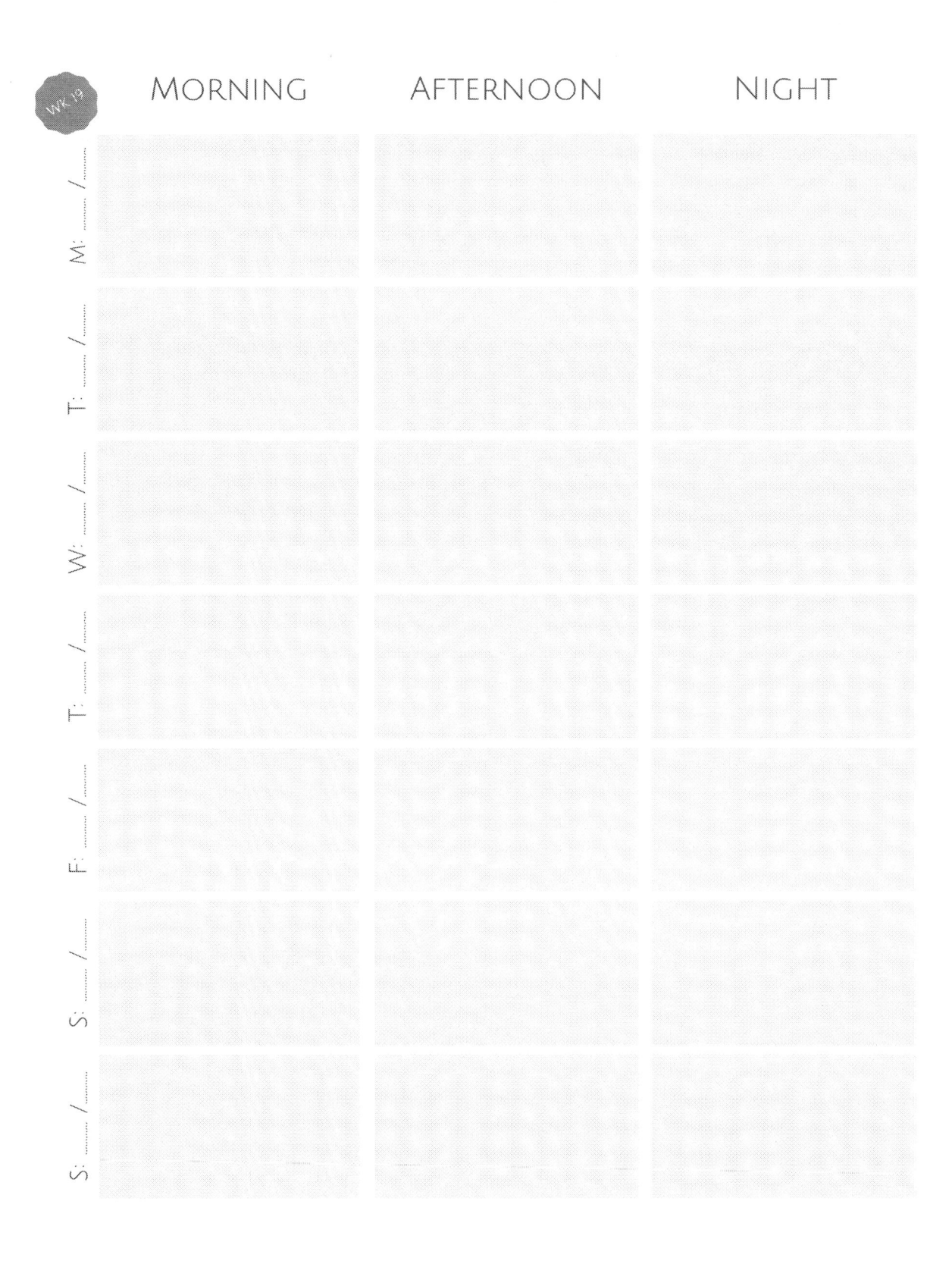

# WRITING PROMPT

*Each writing prompt is optional. If, for whatever reason, it does not speak to you, let it be. Who knows? It might make more sense to do the prompt later in the process.*

Why do you write?

Grab a notebook or open a new document on your computer. Set the timer to 20 minutes and list all the different reasons why you write.

# WEEK 20

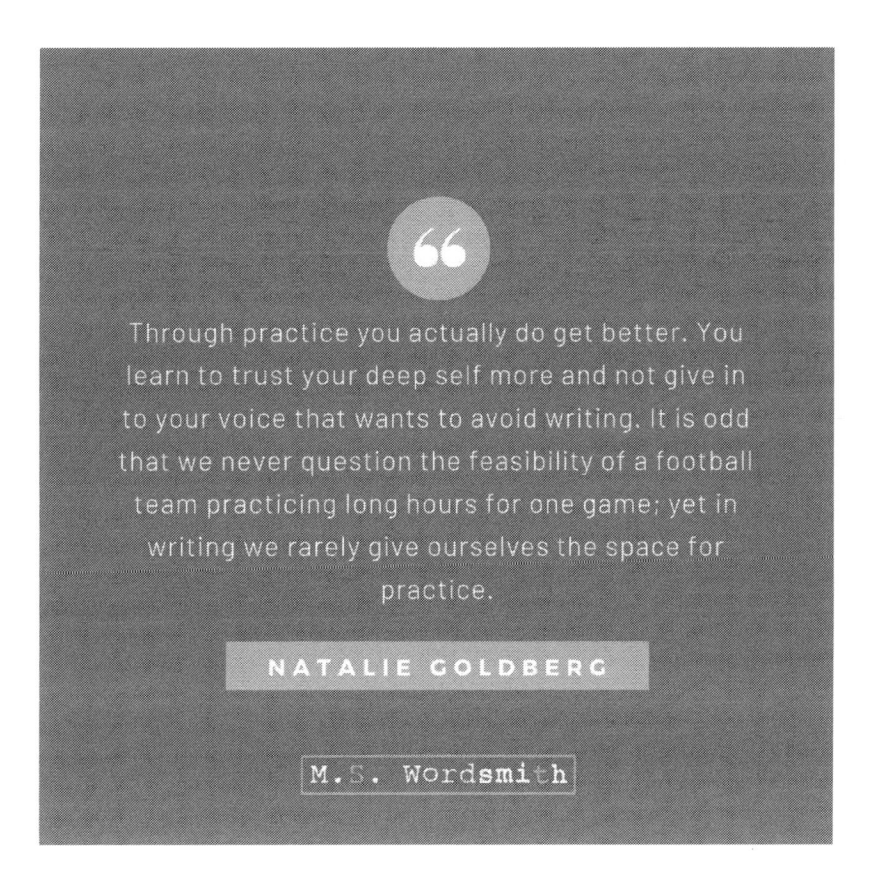

> Through practice you actually do get better. You learn to trust your deep self more and not give in to your voice that wants to avoid writing. It is odd that we never question the feasibility of a football team practicing long hours for one game; yet in writing we rarely give ourselves the space for practice.
>
> — NATALIE GOLDBERG

M.S. Wordsmith

AND JUST LIKE THAT, YOU'VE REACHED WEEK 20!

DATE: ........................................................

# TRACKING

What goal(s) did you set for the past week?

Did you achieve your goal(s)?

WK 20

# Tracking

If yes, did you expect too little of yourself, or was your goal just right? If no, what prevented you from achieving it?

If you didn't reach your goals, what can you do next week to make sure you do?

If you picked an accountability partner last week, was this the right person? What worked and what didn't? Is there anything you'll want to do differently next week?

# PLANNING

What are your goals for the upcoming week?

Have another look. Are you sure this is realistic?
If not, what would be more realistic?

What can you do this week to make sure you achieve your goal(s)?

# Planning

What smaller pieces can you break your goal(s) up into?
Once you're sure you can't break it down anymore, add the sub-goals to the calendar on the next page.

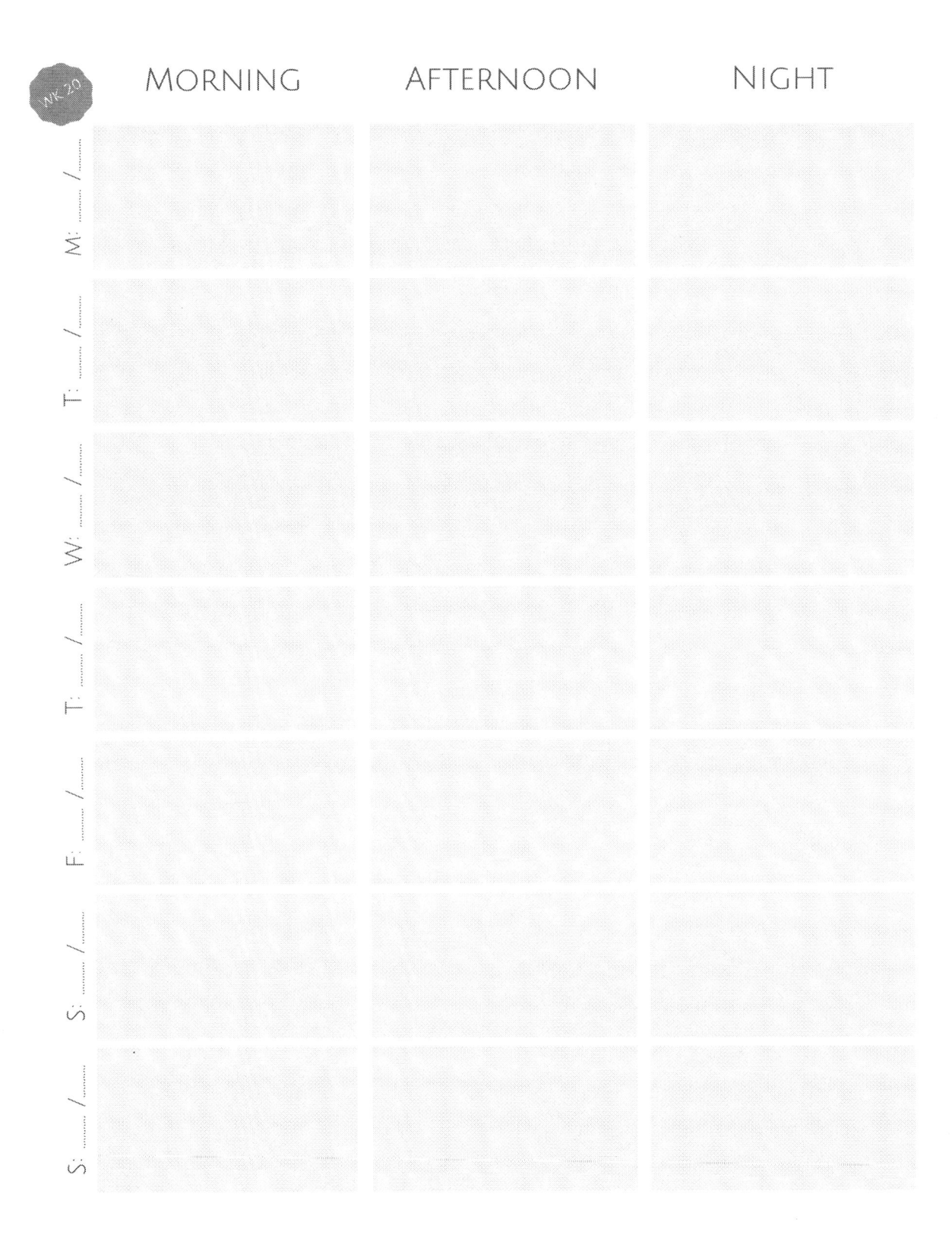

WK 20

|  | MORNING | AFTERNOON | NIGHT |
|---|---|---|---|
| M: / | | | |
| T: / | | | |
| W: / | | | |
| T: / | | | |
| F: / | | | |
| S: / | | | |
| S: / | | | |

# WRITING PROMPT

*Each writing prompt is optional. If, for whatever reason, it does not speak to you, let it be. Who knows? It might make more sense to do the prompt later in the process.*

Do you ever feel like you're not truly writing when not working on your current Work in Progress (WIP)?

This week, just write. Anything. Grow those muscles. So what if the words you get down are not directly related to your current WIP? Practice makes perfect and every little word you write will help you hone your craft.

If you feel like it, grab a notebook or open a new document on your computer at the end of the week and reflect on what you've written and how it made you feel for ten minutes.

# Week 21

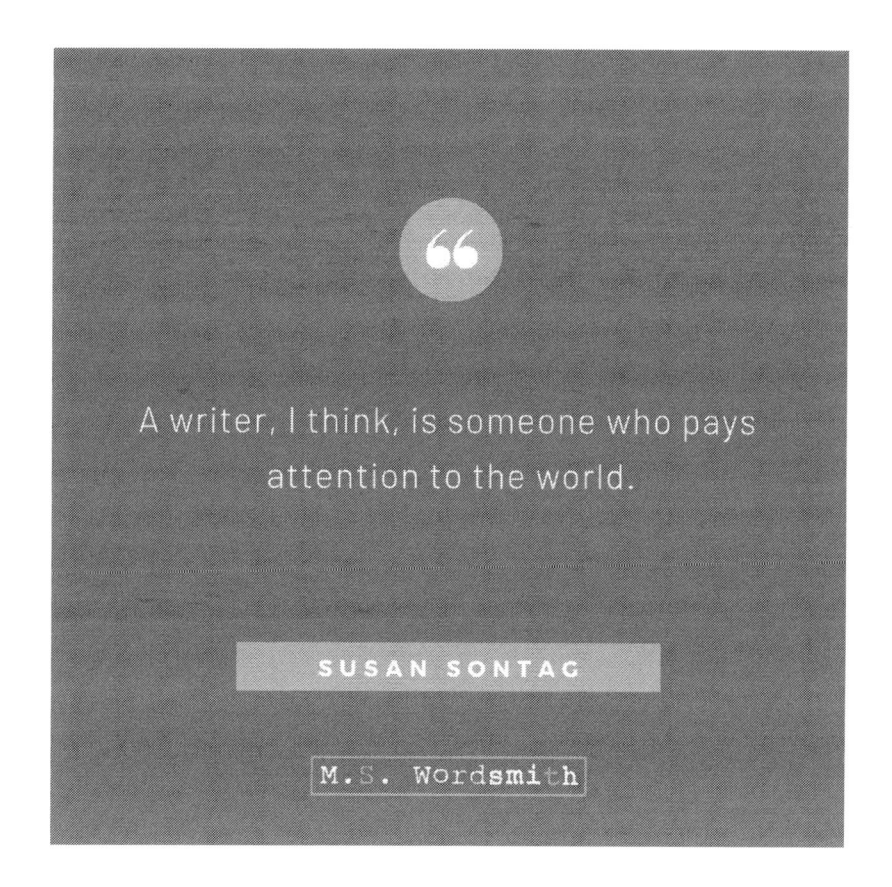

> A writer, I think, is someone who pays attention to the world.
>
> **SUSAN SONTAG**

M.S. Wordsmith

DATE: _____

# Tracking

What goal(s) did you set for the past week?

Did you achieve your goal(s)?

WK 21

# Tracking

If yes, did you expect too little of yourself, or was your goal just right? If no, what prevented you from achieving it?

If you didn't reach your goals, what can you do next week to make sure you do?

If you picked an accountability partner last week, was this the right person? What worked and what didn't? Is there anything you'll want to do differently next week?

# PLANNING

What are your goals for the upcoming week?

Have another look. Are you sure this is realistic?
If not, what would be more realistic?

What can you do this week to make sure you achieve your goal(s)?

WK 21

# Planning

What smaller pieces can you break your goal(s) up into?
Once you're sure you can't break it down anymore, add the sub-goals to the calendar on the next page.

WK 21

| | MORNING | AFTERNOON | NIGHT |
|---|---|---|---|
| M: __/__ | | | |
| T: __/__ | | | |
| W: __/__ | | | |
| T: __/__ | | | |
| F: __/__ | | | |
| S: __/__ | | | |
| S: __/__ | | | |

# WRITING PROMPT

*Each writing prompt is optional. If, for whatever reason, it does not speak to you, let it be. Who knows? It might make more sense to do the prompt later in the process.*

Settle down in front of a window. Set a timer for five minutes, ten minutes, or fifteen – whatever you feel like – and look outside. Just notice. Once the timer goes off, grab your notebook or open a new document on your computer to write down anything that caught your attention.

# Week 22

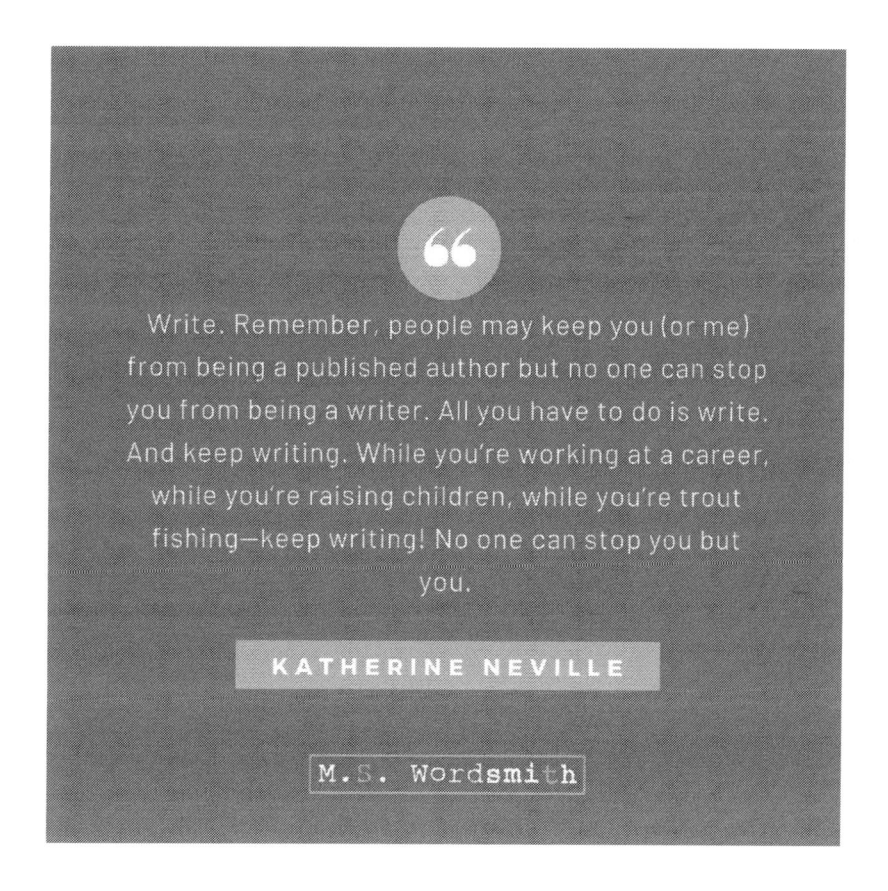

> Write. Remember, people may keep you (or me) from being a published author but no one can stop you from being a writer. All you have to do is write. And keep writing. While you're working at a career, while you're raising children, while you're trout fishing—keep writing! No one can stop you but you.
>
> **KATHERINE NEVILLE**

`M.S. Wordsmith`

IF YOU'VE BEEN DOING THE WRITING PROMPTS, MAKE SURE YOU CARVE OUT TIME FOR THIS WEEK'S AS WELL. IT COULD BE A REAL GAME CHANGER

DATE: _____

# Tracking

What goal(s) did you set for the past week?

Did you achieve your goal(s)?

WK 22

# Tracking

If yes, did you expect too little of yourself, or was your goal just right? If no, what prevented you from achieving it?

If you didn't reach your goals, what can you do next week to make sure you do?

If you picked an accountability partner last week, was this the right person? What worked and what didn't? Is there anything you'll want to do differently next week?

# PLANNING

What are your goals for the upcoming week?

Have another look. Are you sure this is realistic?
If not, what would be more realistic?

What can you do this week to make sure you achieve your goal(s)?

# PLANNING

What smaller pieces can you break your goal(s) up into?
Once you're sure you can't break it down anymore, add the sub-goals to the calendar on the next page.

WK 22

| | MORNING | AFTERNOON | NIGHT |
|---|---|---|---|
| M: / | | | |
| T: / | | | |
| W: / | | | |
| T: / | | | |
| F: / | | | |
| S: / | | | |
| S: / | | | |

# WRITING PROMPT

*Each writing prompt is optional. If, for whatever reason, it does not speak to you, let it be. Who knows? It might make more sense to do the prompt later in the process.*

Do you keep yourself from being a writer sometimes? Is it hard for you to prioritise your writing practice?

Grab a notebook or open a new document on your computer. Set the timer to twenty minutes and list all the things that keep you from writing during the week.

When you're done, sit with each item. Is it truly a priority over writing or is it time you set your priorities straight?

# Week 23

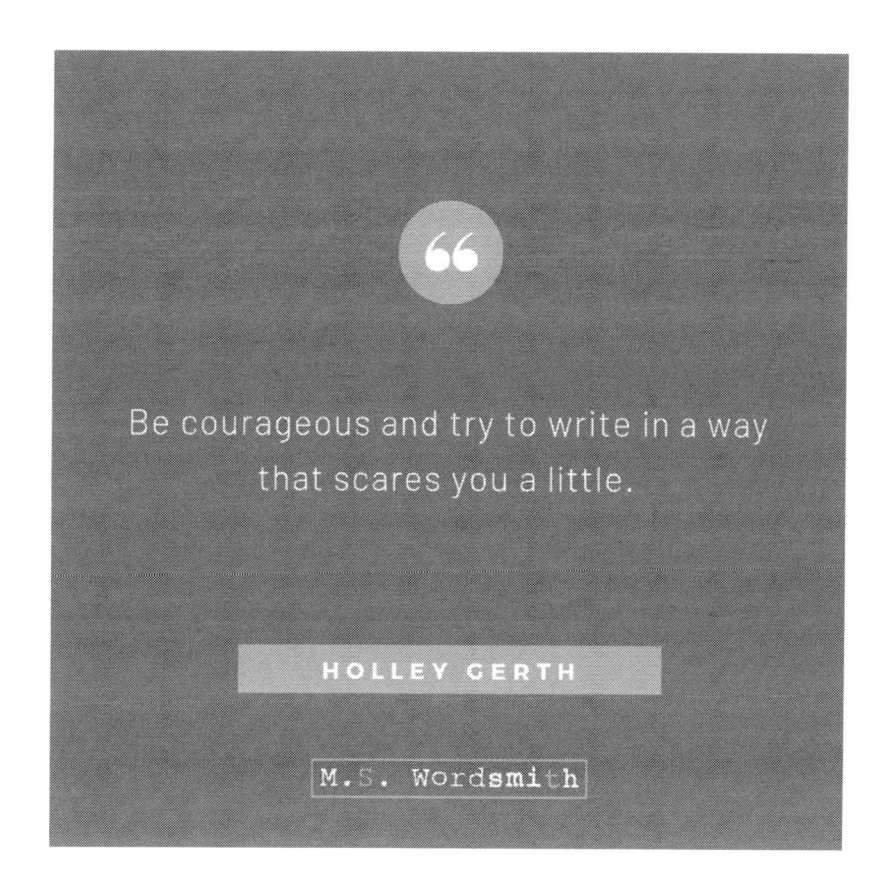

> Be courageous and try to write in a way that scares you a little.
>
> **HOLLEY GERTH**

M.S. Wordsmith

DATE: _____

# Tracking

What goal(s) did you set for the past week?

Did you achieve your goal(s)?

WK 23

# Tracking

If yes, did you expect too little of yourself, or was your goal just right? If no, what prevented you from achieving it?

If you didn't reach your goals, what can you do next week to make sure you do?

If you picked an accountability partner last week, was this the right person? What worked and what didn't? Is there anything you'll want to do differently next week?

# PLANNING

What are your goals for the upcoming week?

Have another look. Are you sure this is realistic?
If not, what would be more realistic?

What can you do this week to make sure you achieve your goal(s)?

WK 23

# PLANNING

What smaller pieces can you break your goal(s) up into?
Once you're sure you can't break it down anymore, add the sub-goals to the calendar on the next page.

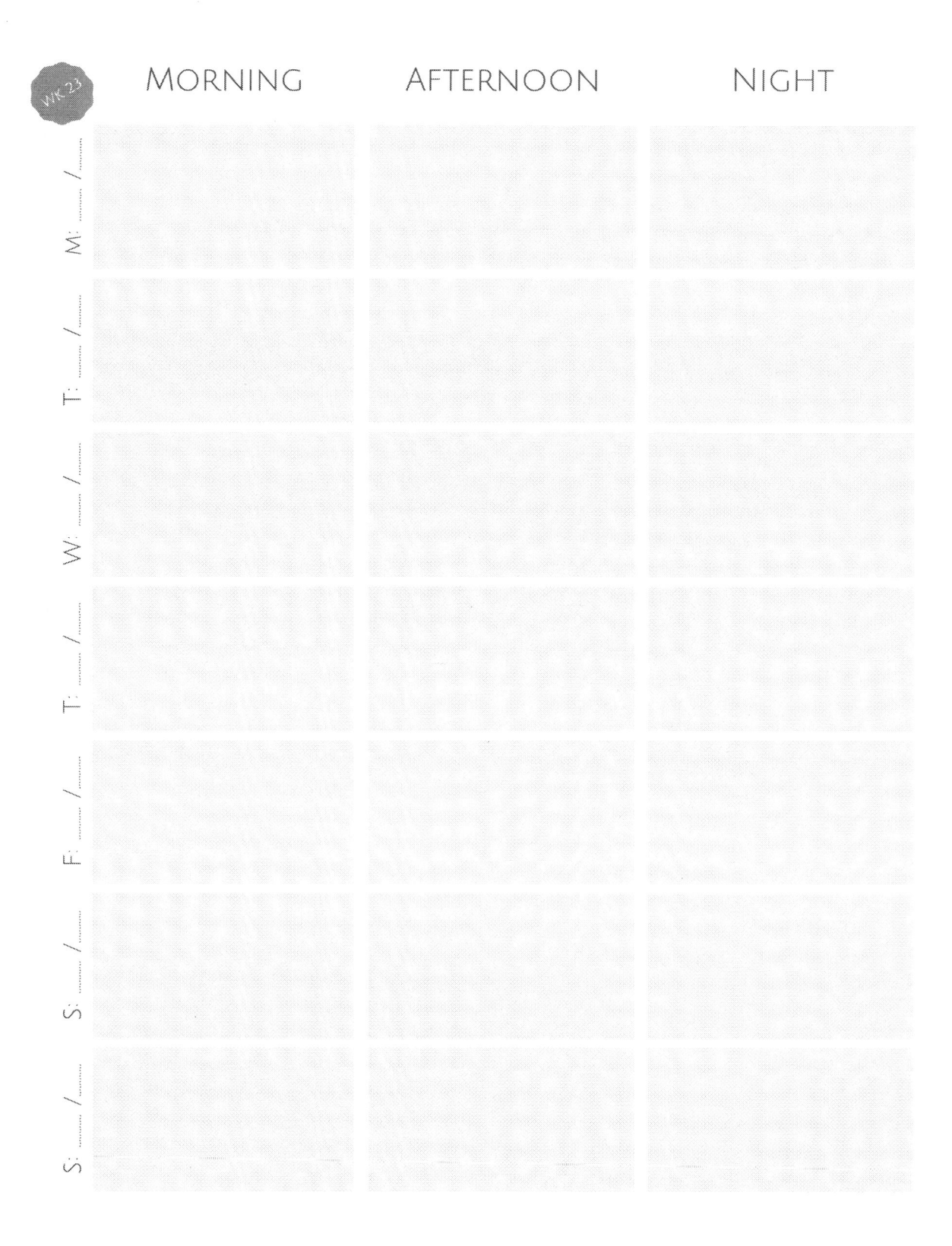

# WK 23

|  | Morning | Afternoon | Night |
|---|---|---|---|
| M: / | | | |
| T: / | | | |
| W: / | | | |
| T: / | | | |
| F: / | | | |
| S: / | | | |
| S: / | | | |

# WRITING PROMPT

*Each writing prompt is optional. If, for whatever reason, it does not speak to you, let it be. Who knows? It might make more sense to do the prompt later in the process.*

Think of that one thing you're afraid to write about. Yes, that's the one, don't push it away, it's too late for that now. You can do this. For five minutes, write about this thing. Just remember to breathe.

# Week 24

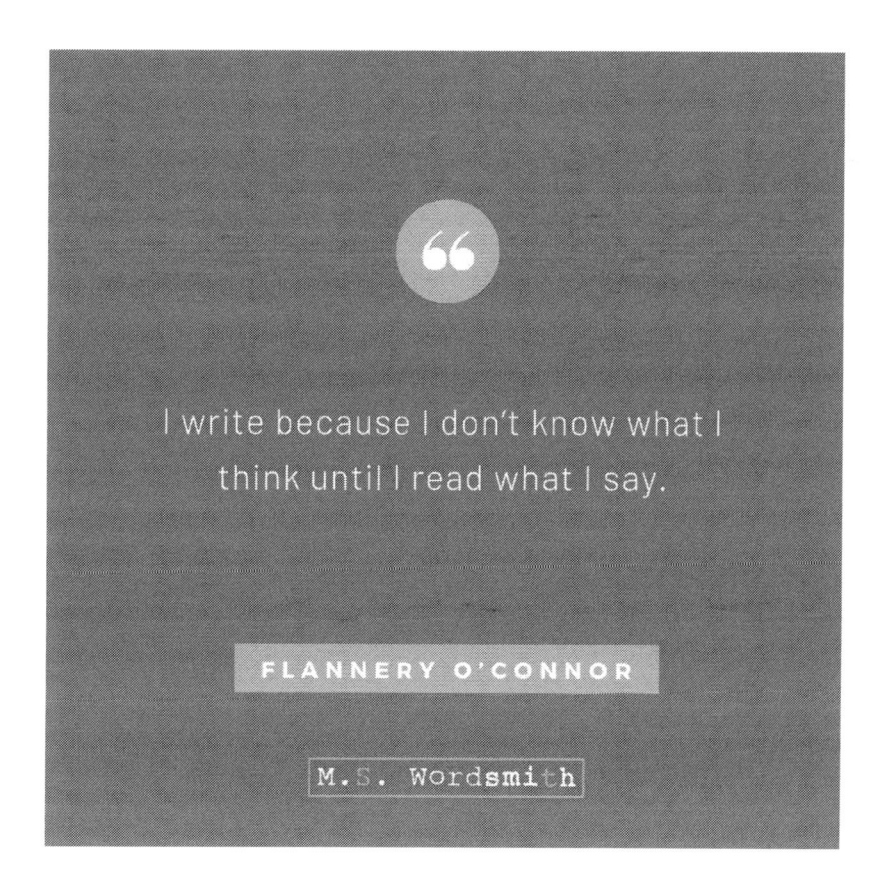

> I write because I don't know what I think until I read what I say.
>
> **FLANNERY O'CONNOR**
>
> M.S. Wordsmith

PSSSST! YOU'VE ALMOST MADE IT THROUGH THE FIRST SIX MONTHS!

DATE: _____

# Tracking

What goal(s) did you set for the past week?

Did you achieve your goal(s)?

WK 24

# Tracking

If yes, did you expect too little of yourself, or was your goal just right? If no, what prevented you from achieving it?

If you didn't reach your goals, what can you do next week to make sure you do?

If you picked an accountability partner last week, was this the right person? What worked and what didn't? Is there anything you'll want to do differently next week?

# PLANNING

What are your goals for the upcoming week?

Have another look. Are you sure this is realistic?
If not, what would be more realistic?

What can you do this week to make sure you achieve your goal(s)?

# PLANNING

What smaller pieces can you break your goal(s) up into?
Once you're sure you can't break it down anymore, add the sub-goals to the calendar on the next page.

WK 24

| | MORNING | AFTERNOON | NIGHT |
|---|---|---|---|
| M: __ / __ | | | |
| T: __ / __ | | | |
| W: __ / __ | | | |
| T: __ / __ | | | |
| F: __ / __ | | | |
| S: __ / __ | | | |
| S: __ / __ | | | |

# Writing Prompt

*Each writing prompt is optional. If, for whatever reason, it does not speak to you, let it be. Who knows? It might make more sense to do the prompt later in the process.*

Take fifteen minutes to free write. Just write, don't look back, just write whatever needs to be written. Try to do this every day for the next seven days. For example, right after you wake up, or when you find yourself stuck in a scene or chapter. Just write whatever comes to you and see if it gets you going or unstuck.

# WEEK 25

> Little by little, one travels far.
>
> J.R.R. TOLKIEN
>
> M.S. Wordsmith

DATE: ........................................

# Tracking

What goal(s) did you set for the past week?

Did you achieve your goal(s)?

WK 25

# Tracking

If yes, did you expect too little of yourself, or was your goal just right? If no, what prevented you from achieving it?

If you didn't reach your goals, what can you do next week to make sure you do?

If you picked an accountability partner last week, was this the right person? What worked and what didn't? Is there anything you'll want to do differently next week?

# PLANNING

What are your goals for the upcoming week?

Have another look. Are you sure this is realistic?
If not, what would be more realistic?

What can you do this week to make sure you achieve your goal(s)?

WK 25

# Planning

What smaller pieces can you break your goal(s) up into?
Once you're sure you can't break it down anymore, add the sub-goals to the calendar on the next page.

WK 25

| | MORNING | AFTERNOON | NIGHT |
|---|---|---|---|
| M: / / | | | |
| T: / / | | | |
| W: / / | | | |
| T: / / | | | |
| F: / / | | | |
| S: / / | | | |
| S: / / | | | |

# WRITING PROMPT

*Each writing prompt is optional. If, for whatever reason, it does not speak to you, let it be. Who knows? It might make more sense to do the prompt later in the process.*

Think of the smallest writing goal you can. This week, every time you hit that goal, you celebrate. How is up to you. Champagne? Chocolate? A long, hot bath? A victory dance in your front garden? Uninterrupted reading time? A yoga class?

# Week 26

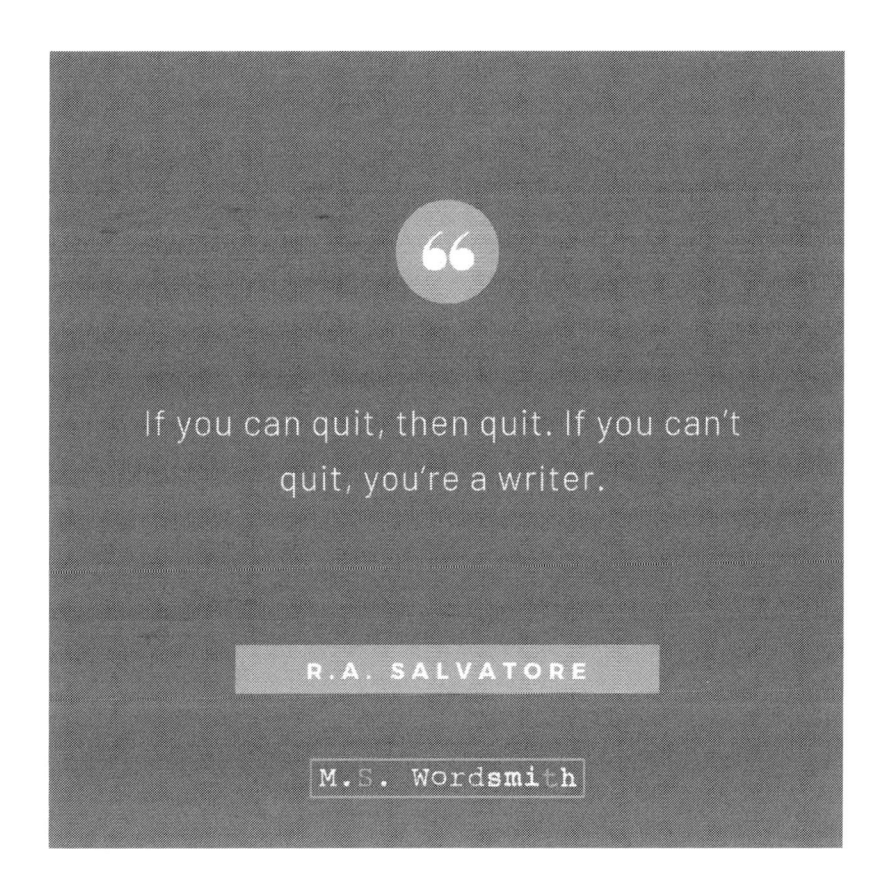

> If you can quit, then quit. If you can't quit, you're a writer.
>
> **R.A. SALVATORE**
>
> M.S. Wordsmith

And...if you're still here, you're definitely a writer. Congrats on reaching the midpoint!

DATE: ............................................................

# Tracking

What goal(s) did you set for the past week?

Did you achieve your goal(s)?

WK 26

# TRACKING

If yes, did you expect too little of yourself, or was your goal just right? If no, what prevented you from achieving it?

If you didn't reach your goals, what can you do next week to make sure you do?

If you picked an accountability partner last week, was this the right person? What worked and what didn't? Is there anything you'll want to do differently next week?

WK 26

# PLANNING

What are your goals for the upcoming week?

Have another look. Are you sure this is realistic?
If not, what would be more realistic?

What can you do this week to make sure you achieve your goal(s)?

# PLANNING

What smaller pieces can you break your goal(s) up into?
Once you're sure you can't break it down anymore, add the sub-goals to the calendar on the next page.

WK 26

| | MORNING | AFTERNOON | NIGHT |
|---|---|---|---|
| M: / | | | |
| T: / | | | |
| W: / | | | |
| T: / | | | |
| F: / | | | |
| S: / | | | |
| S: / | | | |

# Writing Prompt

*Each writing prompt is optional. If, for whatever reason, it does not speak to you, let it be. Who knows? It might make more sense to do the prompt later in the process.*

Could you quit if you wanted to? Imagine you could. What would that be like?

Grab a notebook or open a new document on your computer. Set the timer and take fifteen minutes to answer this question. What would it be like if you would just quit?

Six months and counting!

# How are you going to celebrate?

Write it down, then go do it!

# Week 27

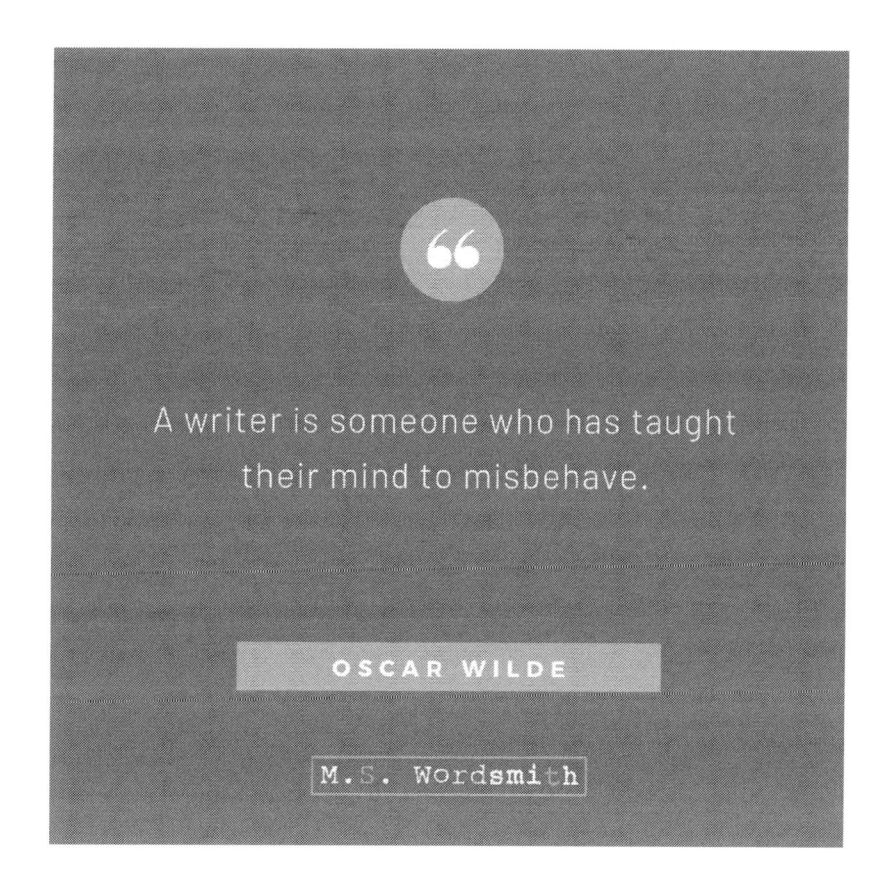

> A writer is someone who has taught their mind to misbehave.
>
> **OSCAR WILDE**
>
> M.S. Wordsmith

DATE: _____

# CLARITY

During Week One, you wrote down why you were first called to write. Over the past three months, have you been able to reconnect to that calling? Take a moment to reflect.

Over the past three months, have you been able to reconnect to how writing used to make you feel? There are no right or wrong answers here. Like the calling, your feelings about writing might have shifted. Take a moment to reflect on this as well.

# CLARITY

Looking back over the past three months, how did the act of writing make you feel? How did you feel right before you started, during, and once you were done?

Are you dealing with the same struggles and roadblocks you identified when we started this journey, or have they changed? If they have, what are you currently struggling with?

# CLARITY

For each struggle and roadblock you are (still) dealing with, can you determine which are internal or external? Even if your list hasn't changed, still reflect on this. Something might very well have shifted in the meantime.

# CLARITY

For each struggle and roadblock, what do you think you need to overcome it? If you're still dealing with the same struggle(s) or roadblock(s), this doesn't mean you didn't make any progress. This is where you get to determine whether you did.

# Reflecting

Let's take a moment to reflect. When looking back on the past three months, what are you most grateful for?

What are the most significant lessons you have learned about yourself and your writing?

Did you achieve your 3-month goal(s)? If yes, (how) did you celebrate? If not, what steps could you take from this week onwards to ensure you reach your next 3-month goal(s)?

WK 27

# GOALS

*Do these goals still hold true or is it time to adjust them?*

Where do you want to be in the next fifty-two weeks? How are you going to celebrate?

In nine months? How are you going to celebrate?

In six months? How are you going to celebrate?

In three months? How are you going to celebrate?

# Tracking

What goal(s) did you set for the past week?

Did you achieve your goal(s)?

WK 27

# TRACKING

If yes, did you expect too little of yourself, or was your goal just right? If no, what prevented you from achieving it?

If you didn't reach your goals, what can you do next week to make sure you do?

If you picked an accountability partner last week, was this the right person? What worked and what didn't? Is there anything you'll want to do differently next week?

# PLANNING

What are your goals for the upcoming week?

Have another look. Are you sure this is realistic?
If not, what would be more realistic?

What can you do this week to make sure you achieve your goal(s)?

WK 27

# Planning

What smaller pieces can you break your goal(s) up into?
Once you're sure you can't break it down anymore, add the sub-goals to the calendar on the next page.

WK 27

|  | MORNING | AFTERNOON | NIGHT |
|---|---|---|---|
| M: __/__ | | | |
| T: __/__ | | | |
| W: __/__ | | | |
| T: __/__ | | | |
| F: __/__ | | | |
| S: __/__ | | | |
| S: __/__ | | | |

WK 27

# Writing prompt

*Each writing prompt is optional. If, for whatever reason, it does not speak to you, let it be. Who knows? It might make more sense to do the prompt later in the process.*

When you talk about your writing, do you separate the writer in you from the rest of you or do you readily acknowledge that, whatever you've written, it's all you?

Make a list of your five favourite authors. Now write down the most horrific, disgusting, troubling, aggravating, naughty, disturbing thing they ever wrote. When you first read these pieces, how did you feel about the author? Did it alter or shape your opinion about them in any big way?

# Week 28

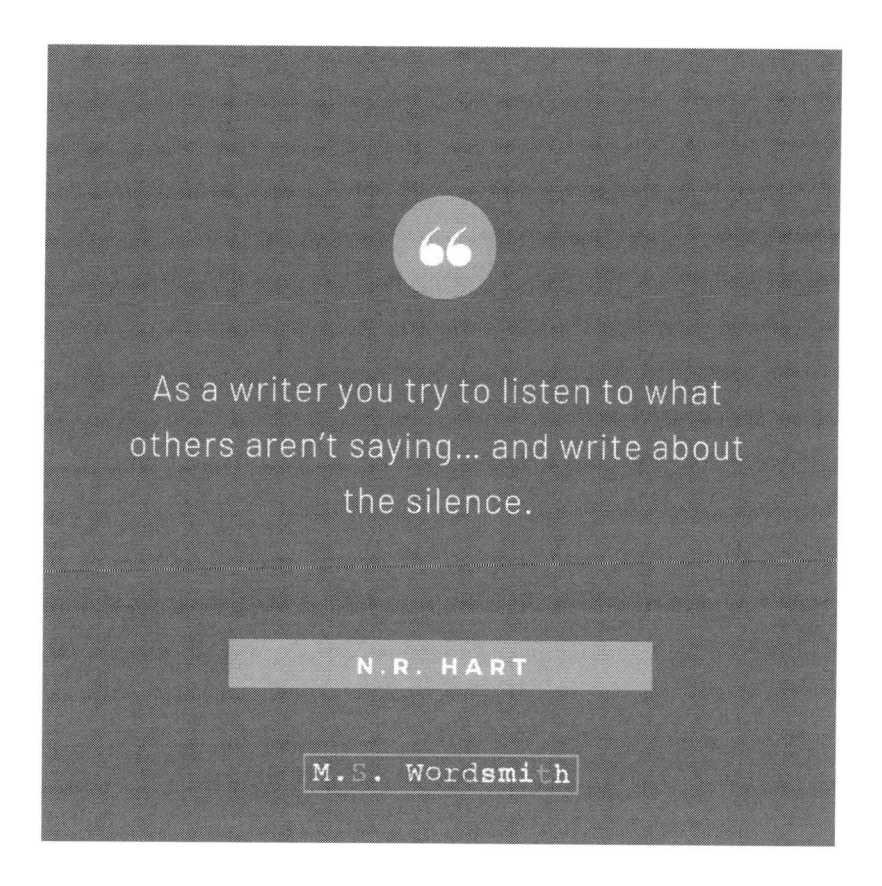

> As a writer you try to listen to what others aren't saying... and write about the silence.
>
> **N.R. HART**

M.S. Wordsmith

I DON'T KNOW ABOUT YOU, BUT I FOR ONE AM GLAD YOU'RE STILL HERE.

DATE: ....................................................

# Tracking

What goal(s) did you set for the past week?

Did you achieve your goal(s)?

# Tracking

If yes, did you expect too little of yourself, or was your goal just right? If no, what prevented you from achieving it?

If you didn't reach your goals, what can you do next week to make sure you do?

If you picked an accountability partner last week, was this the right person? What worked and what didn't? Is there anything you'll want to do differently next week?

# PLANNING

What are your goals for the upcoming week?

Have another look. Are you sure this is realistic?
If not, what would be more realistic?

What can you do this week to make sure you achieve your goal(s)?

WK 28

# PLANNING

What smaller pieces can you break your goal(s) up into?
Once you're sure you can't break it down anymore, add the sub-goals to the calendar on the next page.

WK 28

|  | Morning | Afternoon | Night |
|---|---|---|---|
| M: __/__ | | | |
| T: __/__ | | | |
| W: __/__ | | | |
| T: __/__ | | | |
| F: __/__ | | | |
| S: __/__ | | | |
| S: __/__ | | | |

Wk 28

# WRITING PROMPT

*Each writing prompt is optional. If, for whatever reason, it does not speak to you, let it be. Who knows? It might make more sense to do the prompt later in the process.*

Grab a notebook or open a new document on your computer and write a scene in which the little gestures, the facial expressions, and the silences say it all, and not the actual dialogue.

# Week 29

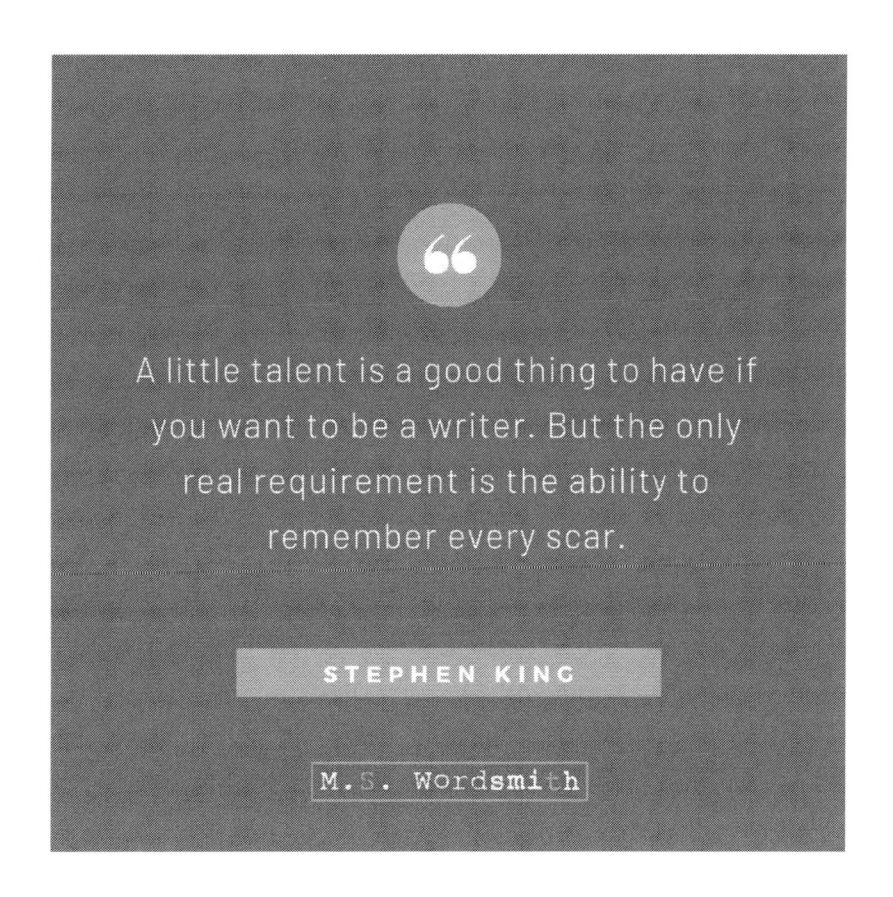

> "A little talent is a good thing to have if you want to be a writer. But the only real requirement is the ability to remember every scar."
>
> **STEPHEN KING**
>
> M.S. Wordsmith

Date: ...........................................................

# TRACKING

What goal(s) did you set for the past week?

Did you achieve your goal(s)?

WK 29

# TRACKING

If yes, did you expect too little of yourself, or was your goal just right? If no, what prevented you from achieving it?

If you didn't reach your goals, what can you do next week to make sure you do?

If you picked an accountability partner last week, was this the right person? What worked and what didn't? Is there anything you'll want to do differently next week?

# PLANNING

What are your goals for the upcoming week?

Have another look. Are you sure this is realistic?
If not, what would be more realistic?

What can you do this week to make sure you achieve your goal(s)?

# PLANNING

What smaller pieces can you break your goal(s) up into?
Once you're sure you can't break it down anymore, add the sub-goals to the calendar on the next page.

WK 29

WK 29

|  | MORNING | AFTERNOON | NIGHT |
|---|---|---|---|
| M: / | | | |
| T: / | | | |
| W: / | | | |
| T: / | | | |
| F: / | | | |
| S: / | | | |
| S: / | | | |

# Writing Prompt

*Each writing prompt is optional. If, for whatever reason, it does not speak to you, let it be. Who knows? It might make more sense to do the prompt later in the process.*

Look closely at your body and find the little scars that have been a part of you for as long as you remember. How did they get there?

Grab a notebook or open a new document on your computer and take fifteen minutes or as long as you need to tell the story from A to Z.

# Week 30

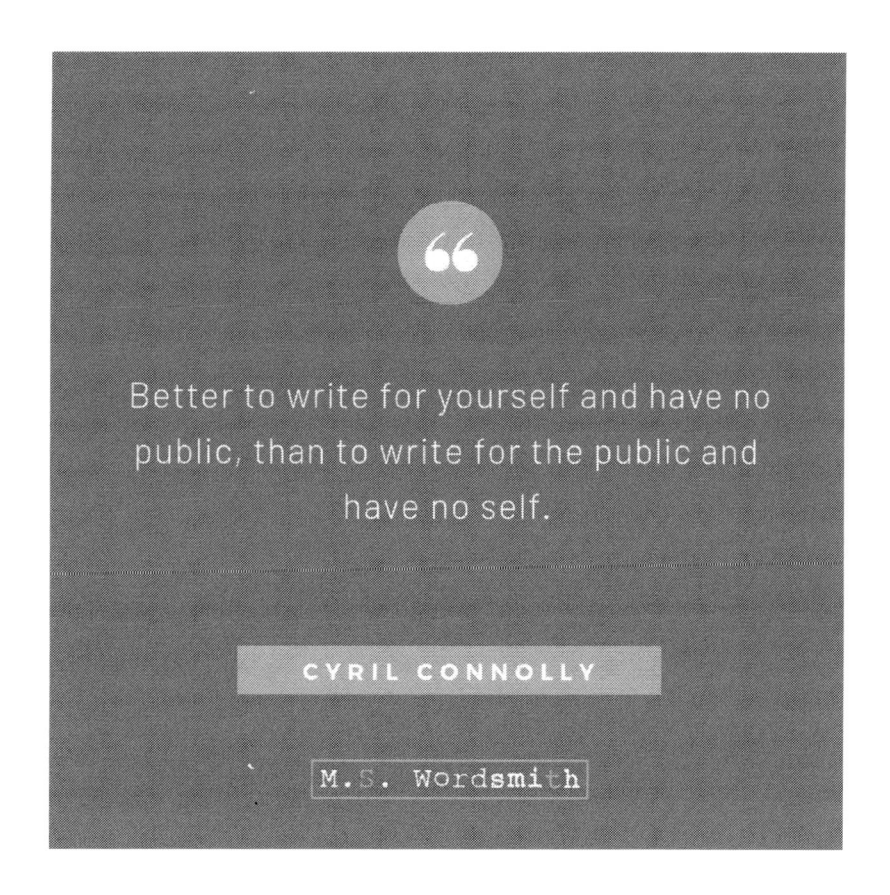

> Better to write for yourself and have no public, than to write for the public and have no self.
>
> **CYRIL CONNOLLY**

M.S. Wordsmith

WHO ARE YOU WRITING FOR? DO YOU HAVE AN AUDIENCE OR DO YOU KEEP EVERYTHING TO YOURSELF?

DATE: _____

# Tracking

What goal(s) did you set for the past week?

Did you achieve your goal(s)?

WK 30

# Tracking

If yes, did you expect too little of yourself, or was your goal just right? If no, what prevented you from achieving it?

If you didn't reach your goals, what can you do next week to make sure you do?

If you picked an accountability partner last week, was this the right person? What worked and what didn't? Is there anything you'll want to do differently next week?

# PLANNING

What are your goals for the upcoming week?

Have another look. Are you sure this is realistic?
If not, what would be more realistic?

What can you do this week to make sure you achieve your goal(s)?

# PLANNING

What smaller pieces can you break your goal(s) up into?
Once you're sure you can't break it down anymore, add the sub-goals to the calendar on the next page.

WK 30

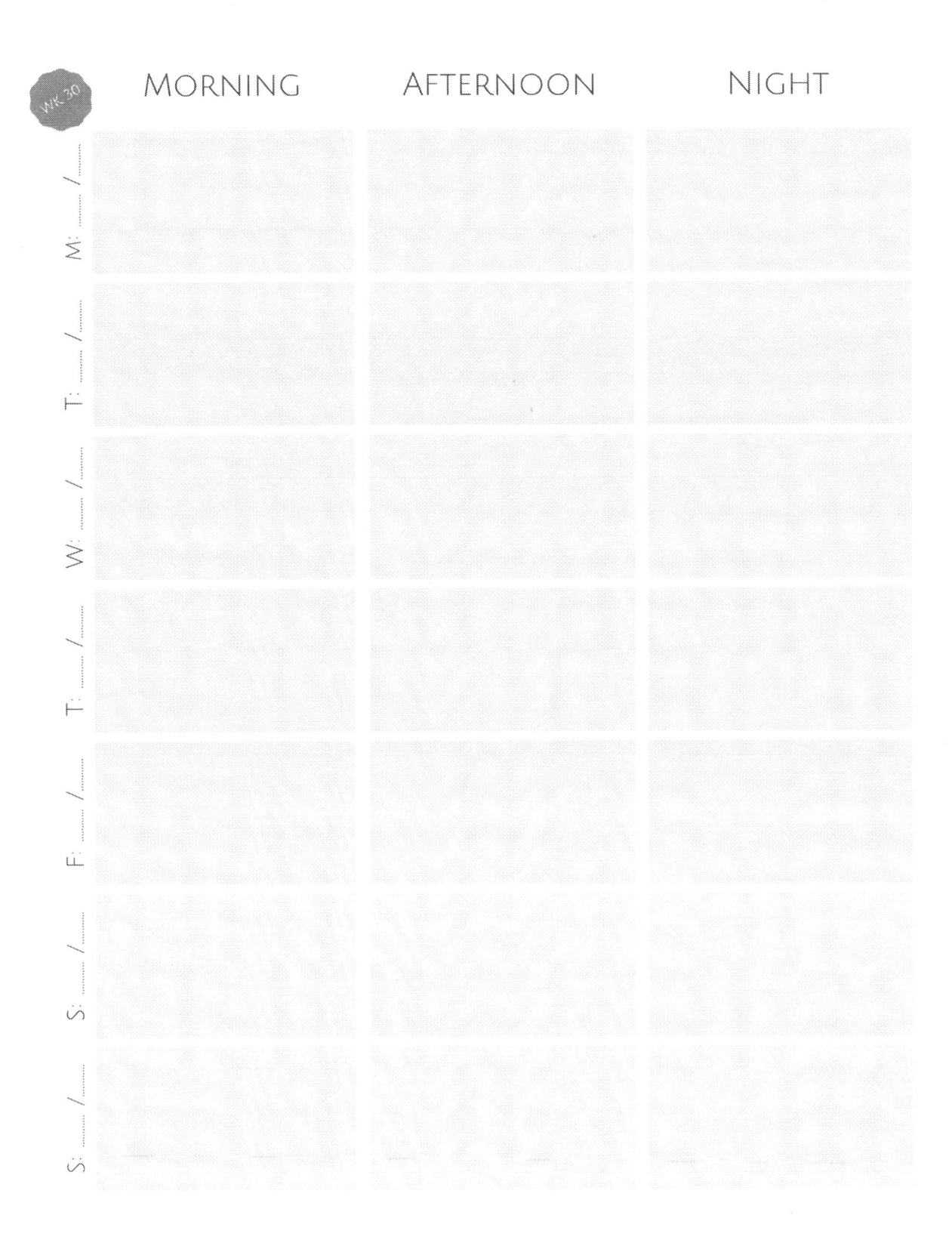

| | MORNING | AFTERNOON | NIGHT |
|---|---|---|---|
| M: __ / __ | | | |
| T: __ / __ | | | |
| W: __ / __ | | | |
| T: __ / __ | | | |
| F: __ / __ | | | |
| S: __ / __ | | | |
| S: __ / __ | | | |

# WRITING PROMPT

*Each writing prompt is optional. If, for whatever reason, it does not speak to you, let it be. Who knows? It might make more sense to do the prompt later in the process.*

In *On Writing: A Memoir of the Craft*, Stephen King talks about the Ideal Reader, the one person you write for. While not everyone has one Ideal Reader, most of us know who we don't want to read our work.

Take a moment to write their names down. If there are a lot, pick the three most important ones. Now grab a notebook or open a new document on your computer. Take fifteen minutes per person to write them a letter explaining why, from this moment on, you will no longer regard their opinion of you or your work.

# Week 31

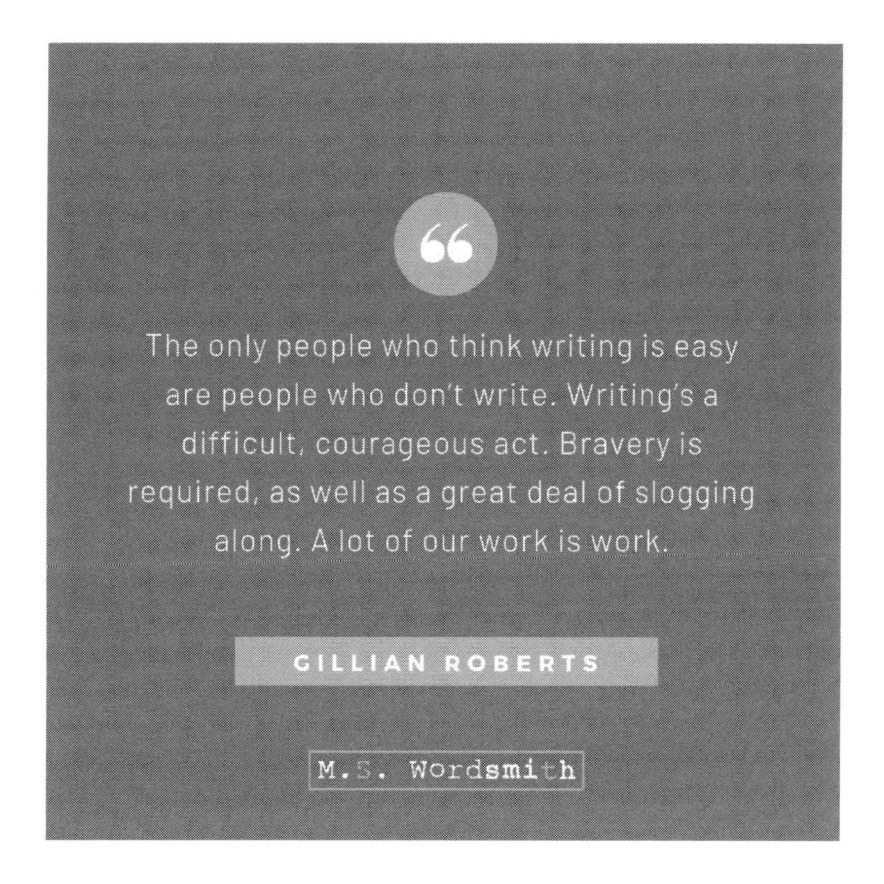

> The only people who think writing is easy are people who don't write. Writing's a difficult, courageous act. Bravery is required, as well as a great deal of slogging along. A lot of our work is work.
>
> **GILLIAN ROBERTS**
>
> M.S. Wordsmith

DATE: ..........................................................

# Tracking

What goal(s) did you set for the past week?

Did you achieve your goal(s)?

WK 31

# Tracking

If yes, did you expect too little of yourself, or was your goal just right? If no, what prevented you from achieving it?

If you didn't reach your goals, what can you do next week to make sure you do?

If you picked an accountability partner last week, was this the right person? What worked and what didn't? Is there anything you'll want to do differently next week?

# PLANNING

What are your goals for the upcoming week?

Have another look. Are you sure this is realistic?
If not, what would be more realistic?

What can you do this week to make sure you achieve your goal(s)?

WK 31

# PLANNING

What smaller pieces can you break your goal(s) up into?
Once you're sure you can't break it down anymore, add the sub-goals to the calendar on the next page.

|  | Morning | Afternoon | Night |
|---|---|---|---|
| Wk 31 | | | |
| M: / | | | |
| T: / | | | |
| W: / | | | |
| T: / | | | |
| F: / | | | |
| S: / | | | |
| S: / | | | |

# WRITING PROMPT

*Each writing prompt is optional. If, for whatever reason, it does not speak to you, let it be. Who knows? It might make more sense to do the prompt later in the process.*

Other people's misunderstandings about writing can be rather crippling. However, what other people think will never be as crippling as some of the stories we tell ourselves about our writing practice.

Grab a notebook or open a new document on your computer. Set the timer to twenty minutes and write a manifesto for yourself, something you can pin to your wall once you're finished, starting with the words 'I am courageous because I write. I am brave because I write'.

# Week 32

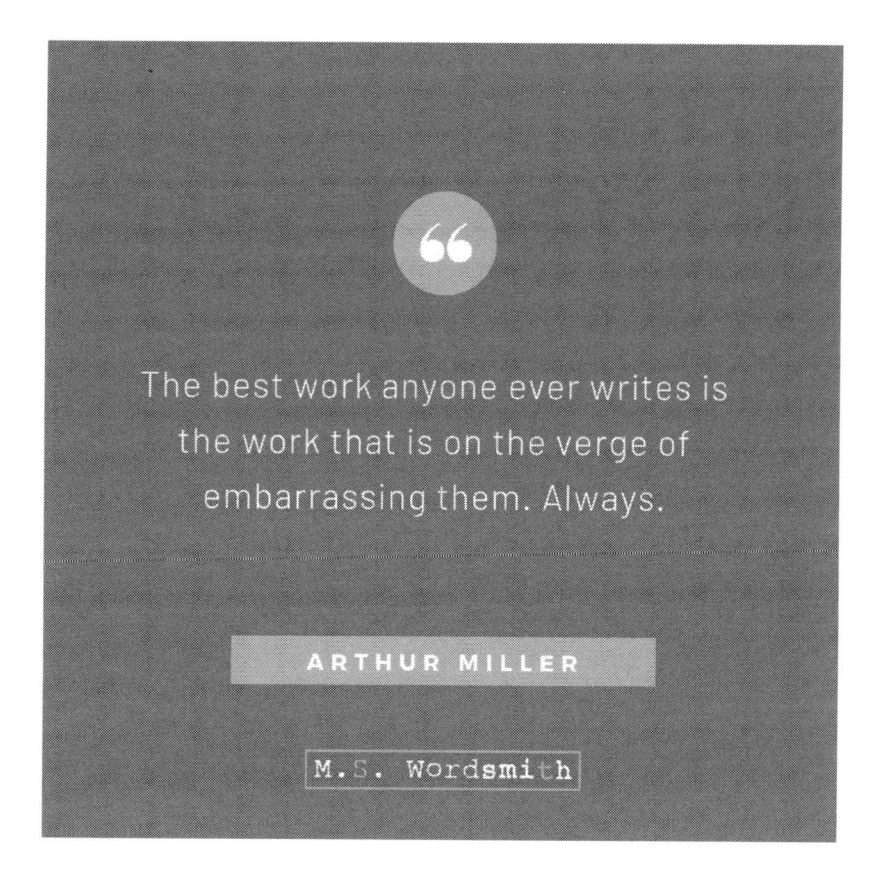

> The best work anyone ever writes is the work that is on the verge of embarrassing them. Always.
>
> **ARTHUR MILLER**
>
> M.S. Wordsmith

ARE YOU READY TO DIG DEEP THIS WEEK?

DATE: _____

# TRACKING

What goal(s) did you set for the past week?

Did you achieve your goal(s)?

WK 32

# Tracking

If yes, did you expect too little of yourself, or was your goal just right? If no, what prevented you from achieving it?

If you didn't reach your goals, what can you do next week to make sure you do?

If you picked an accountability partner last week, was this the right person? What worked and what didn't? Is there anything you'll want to do differently next week?

# PLANNING

What are your goals for the upcoming week?

Have another look. Are you sure this is realistic?
If not, what would be more realistic?

What can you do this week to make sure you achieve your goal(s)?

WK 32

# PLANNING

What smaller pieces can you break your goal(s) up into?
Once you're sure you can't break it down anymore, add the sub-goals to the calendar on the next page.

WK 32

WK 32

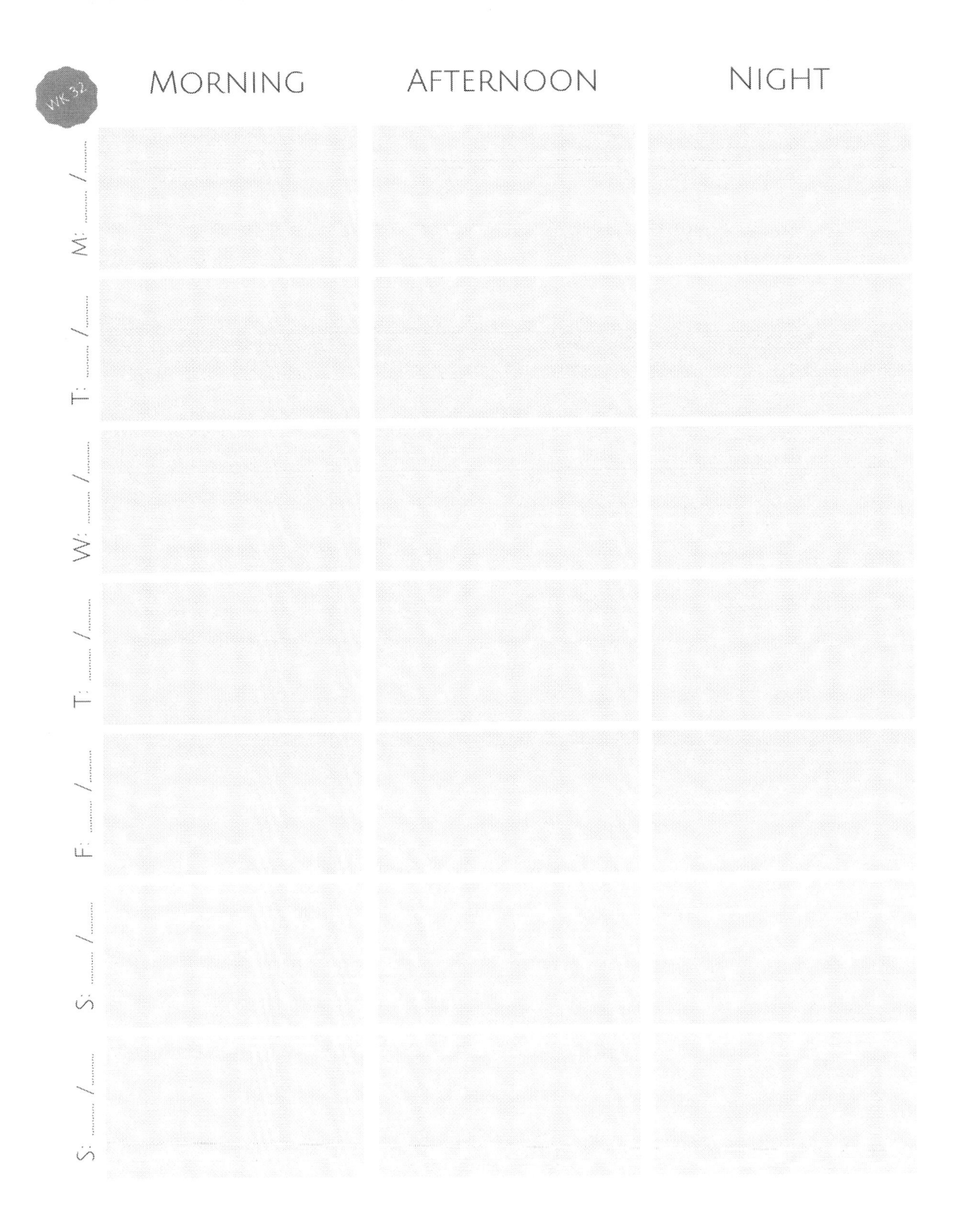

| | MORNING | AFTERNOON | NIGHT |
|---|---|---|---|
| M: __/__ | | | |
| T: __/__ | | | |
| W: __/__ | | | |
| T: __/__ | | | |
| F: __/__ | | | |
| S: __/__ | | | |
| S: __/__ | | | |

# WRITING PROMPT

*Each writing prompt is optional. If, for whatever reason, it does not speak to you, let it be. Who knows? It might make more sense to do the prompt later in the process.*

Grab a notebook or open a new document on your computer. Set the timer to twenty minutes and write something you'd be scared for a loved one to find, whether it's someone who raised you, a friend, your spouse.

# Week 33

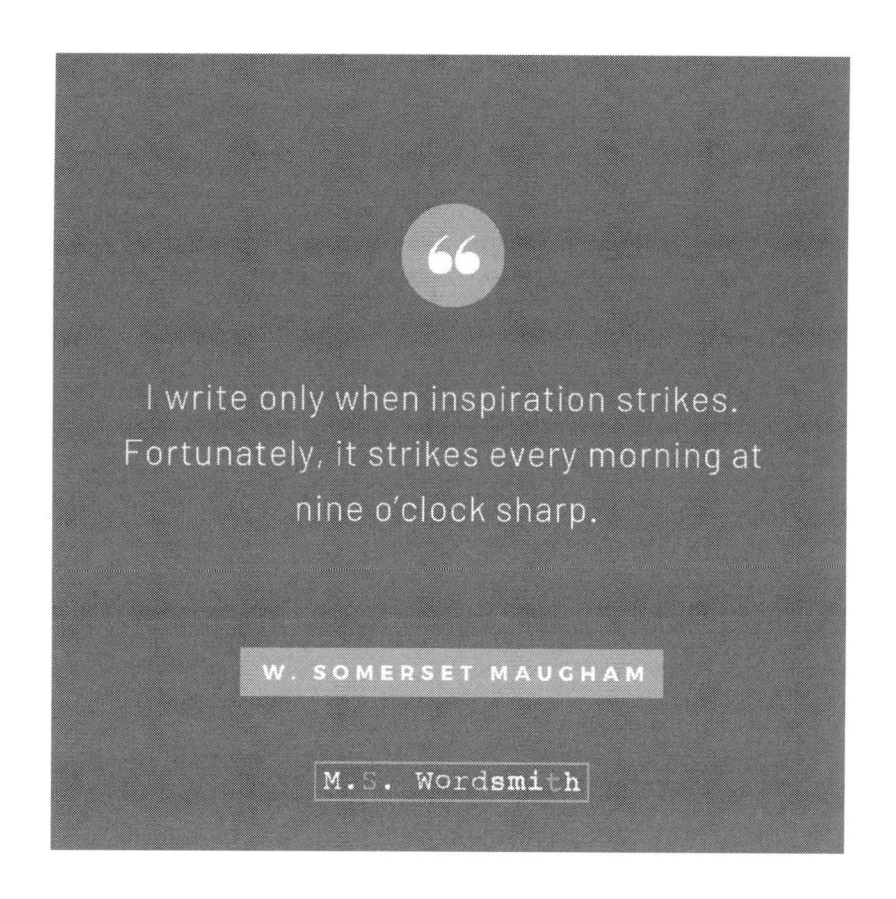

> I write only when inspiration strikes. Fortunately, it strikes every morning at nine o'clock sharp.

**W. SOMERSET MAUGHAM**

M.S. Wordsmith

DATE: ...................................................................

# Tracking

What goal(s) did you set for the past week?

Did you achieve your goal(s)?

WK 33

# Tracking

If yes, did you expect too little of yourself, or was your goal just right? If no, what prevented you from achieving it?

If you didn't reach your goals, what can you do next week to make sure you do?

If you picked an accountability partner last week, was this the right person? What worked and what didn't? Is there anything you'll want to do differently next week?

# PLANNING

What are your goals for the upcoming week?

Have another look. Are you sure this is realistic?
If not, what would be more realistic?

What can you do this week to make sure you achieve your goal(s)?

# PLANNING

What smaller pieces can you break your goal(s) up into?
Once you're sure you can't break it down anymore, add the sub-goals to the calendar on the next page.

WK 33

WK 33

|  | MORNING | AFTERNOON | NIGHT |
|---|---|---|---|
| M: / | | | |
| T: / | | | |
| W: / | | | |
| T: / | | | |
| F: / | | | |
| S: / | | | |
| S: / | | | |

# Writing prompt

*Each writing prompt is optional. If, for whatever reason, it does not speak to you, let it be. Who knows? It might make more sense to do the prompt later in the process.*

Do you know what time works best for you when it comes to writing? This week, try to write at different times and see what shows up for you. You might be surprised.

# Week 34

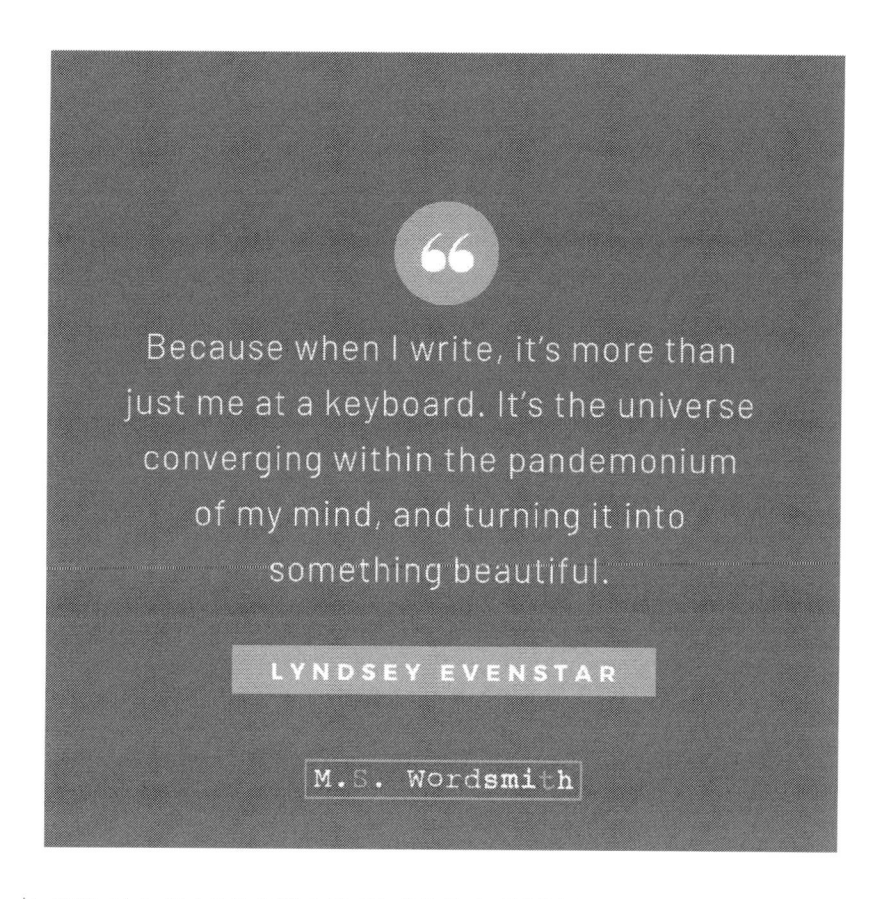

> Because when I write, it's more than just me at a keyboard. It's the universe converging within the pandemonium of my mind, and turning it into something beautiful.
>
> **LYNDSEY EVENSTAR**
>
> `M.S. Wordsmith`

JUST IN CASE YOU'VE BEEN FEELING OTHERWISE: YOU'VE GOT THIS!

DATE: _____

# TRACKING

What goal(s) did you set for the past week?

Did you achieve your goal(s)?

WK 34

# TRACKING

If yes, did you expect too little of yourself, or was your goal just right? If no, what prevented you from achieving it?

If you didn't reach your goals, what can you do next week to make sure you do?

If you picked an accountability partner last week, was this the right person? What worked and what didn't? Is there anything you'll want to do differently next week?

# PLANNING

What are your goals for the upcoming week?

Have another look. Are you sure this is realistic?
If not, what would be more realistic?

What can you do this week to make sure you achieve your goal(s)?

# PLANNING

What smaller pieces can you break your goal(s) up into?
Once you're sure you can't break it down anymore, add the sub-goals to the calendar on the next page.

WK 34

WK. 34

| | MORNING | AFTERNOON | NIGHT |
|---|---|---|---|
| M: __/__ | | | |
| T: __/__ | | | |
| W: __/__ | | | |
| T: __/__ | | | |
| F: __/__ | | | |
| S: __/__ | | | |
| S: __/__ | | | |

# WRITING PROMPT

*Each writing prompt is optional. If, for whatever reason, it does not speak to you, let it be. Who knows? It might make more sense to do the prompt later in the process.*

Do you remember the last time you were writing and it all came together? What piece were you working on? Take a moment to reread what you did there. Can you pinpoint what makes this piece just right?

If you can't, don't worry. Ask a friend or a writing buddy to have a look as well. Perhaps you can figure it out together.

# Week 35

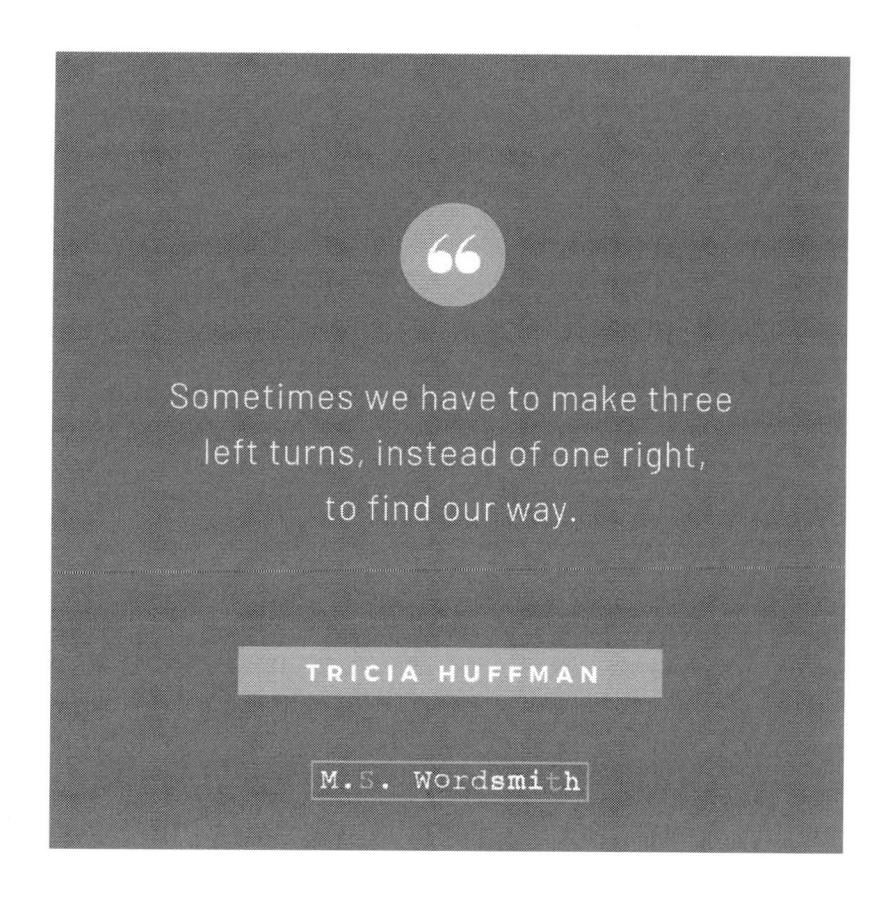

> Sometimes we have to make three left turns, instead of one right, to find our way.
>
> **TRICIA HUFFMAN**

`M.S. Wordsmith`

DATE: _____

# TRACKING

What goal(s) did you set for the past week?

Did you achieve your goal(s)?

WK 35

# Tracking

If yes, did you expect too little of yourself, or was your goal just right? If no, what prevented you from achieving it?

If you didn't reach your goals, what can you do next week to make sure you do?

If you picked an accountability partner last week, was this the right person? What worked and what didn't? Is there anything you'll want to do differently next week?

WK 35

# PLANNING

What are your goals for the upcoming week?

Have another look. Are you sure this is realistic?
If not, what would be more realistic?

What can you do this week to make sure you achieve your goal(s)?

WK 35

# PLANNING

What smaller pieces can you break your goal(s) up into?
Once you're sure you can't break it down anymore, add the sub-goals to the calendar on the next page.

WK 35

| | MORNING | AFTERNOON | NIGHT |
|---|---|---|---|
| M: / | | | |
| T: / | | | |
| W: / | | | |
| T: / | | | |
| F: / | | | |
| S: / | | | |
| S: / | | | |

# WRITING PROMPT

*Each writing prompt is optional. If, for whatever reason, it does not speak to you, let it be. Who knows? It might make more sense to do the prompt later in the process.*

Do you suffer from comparisonitis? Are you constantly checking what other people are doing and comparing it to your own goals, progress, ways?

Grab a notebook or open a new document on your computer. Set the timer to ten minutes and write down what you think your writing practice should be like.

Once you're done, reset the timer and write down what you would love your writing practice to look like.

Compare notes. Does anything stand out?

# Week 36

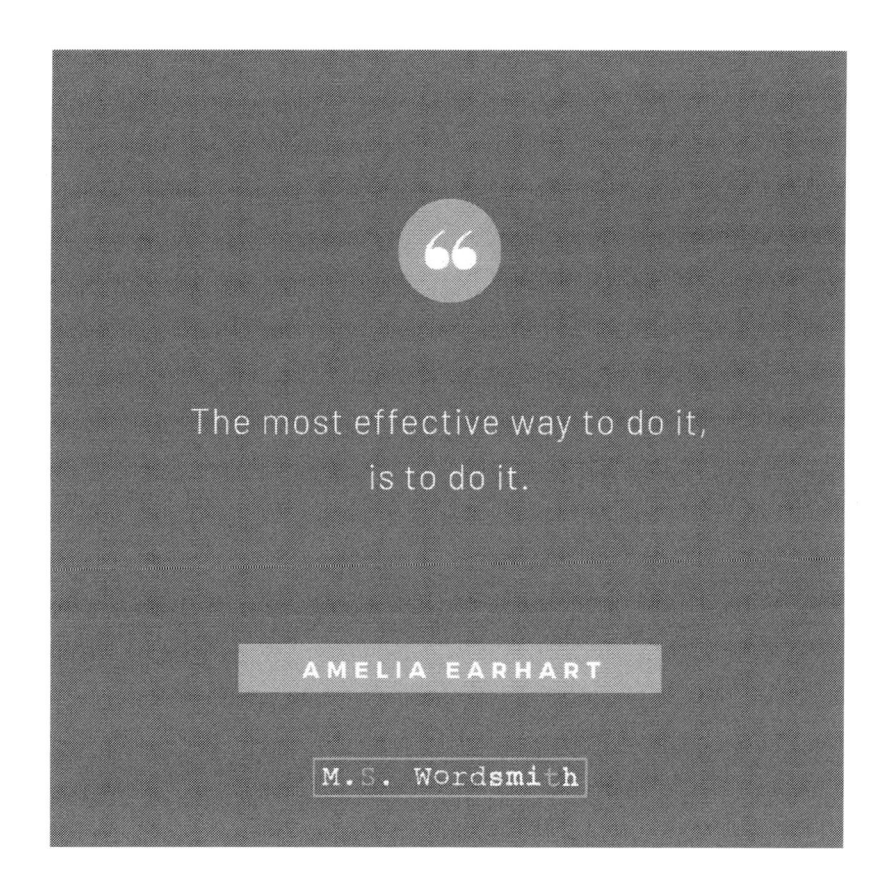

> The most effective way to do it,
> is to do it.
>
> **AMELIA EARHART**
>
> M.S. Wordsmith

Can you believe there are only sixteen more weeks to go? Cheers to that!

DATE: ..................................................

# Tracking

What goal(s) did you set for the past week?

Did you achieve your goal(s)?

WK 36

# TRACKING

If yes, did you expect too little of yourself, or was your goal just right? If no, what prevented you from achieving it?

If you didn't reach your goals, what can you do next week to make sure you do?

If you picked an accountability partner last week, was this the right person? What worked and what didn't? Is there anything you'll want to do differently next week?

# PLANNING

What are your goals for the upcoming week?

Have another look. Are you sure this is realistic?
If not, what would be more realistic?

What can you do this week to make sure you achieve your goal(s)?

WK 36

# PLANNING

What smaller pieces can you break your goal(s) up into?
Once you're sure you can't break it down anymore, add the sub-goals to the calendar on the next page.

# WK 36

|   | Morning | Afternoon | Night |
|---|---------|-----------|-------|
| M: __ / __ | | | |
| T: __ / __ | | | |
| W: __ / __ | | | |
| T: __ / __ | | | |
| F: __ / __ | | | |
| S: __ / __ | | | |
| S: __ / __ | | | |

# WRITING PROMPT

*Each writing prompt is optional. If, for whatever reason, it does not speak to you, let it be. Who knows? It might make more sense to do the prompt later in the process.*

Look at the different elements you uncovered during Week Nineteen.

Set the timer to twenty minutes and turn whatever you wrote down then into a concise list of 'Reasons to Write'. Expand where necessary but try to keep it short so you can keep this list with you at all times, for example on a post-it in your wallet or purse. Whenever the reluctance is strong, reread your list until you're ready to write.

# WEEK 37

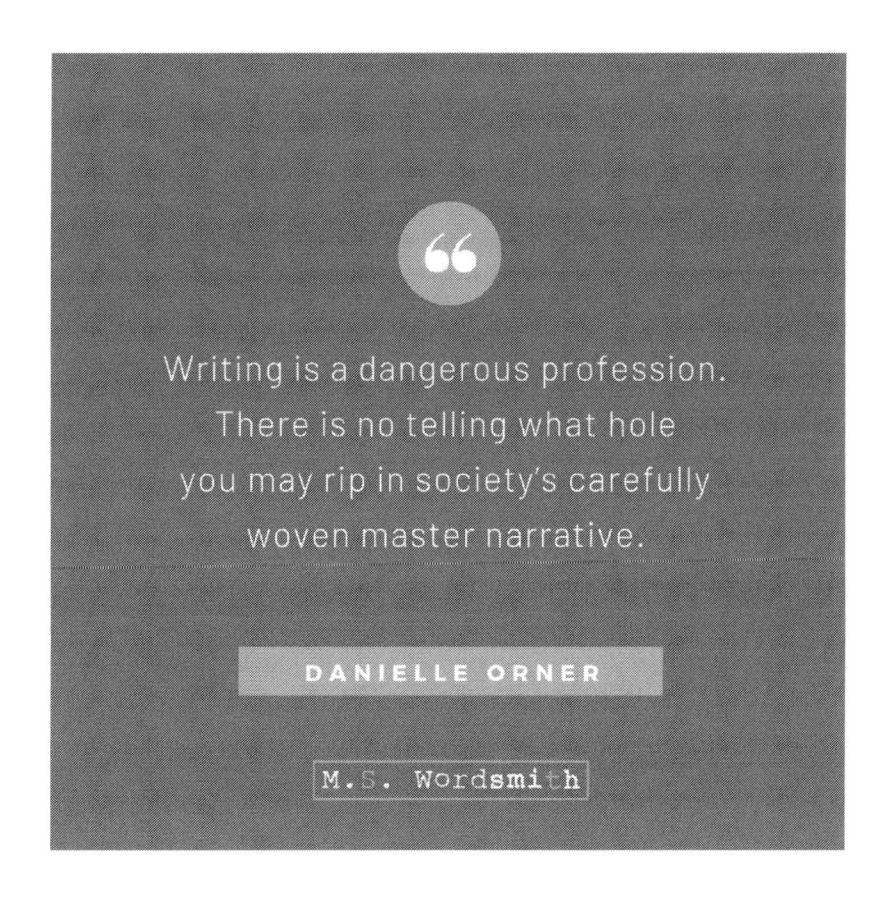

> Writing is a dangerous profession. There is no telling what hole you may rip in society's carefully woven master narrative.
>
> **DANIELLE ORNER**
>
> M.S. Wordsmith

DATE: ...........................................................

# TRACKING

What goal(s) did you set for the past week?

Did you achieve your goal(s)?

WK 37

# TRACKING

If yes, did you expect too little of yourself, or was your goal just right? If no, what prevented you from achieving it?

If you didn't reach your goals, what can you do next week to make sure you do?

If you picked an accountability partner last week, was this the right person? What worked and what didn't? Is there anything you'll want to do differently next week?

# PLANNING

What are your goals for the upcoming week?

Have another look. Are you sure this is realistic?
If not, what would be more realistic?

What can you do this week to make sure you achieve your goal(s)?

# Planning

What smaller pieces can you break your goal(s) up into?
Once you're sure you can't break it down anymore, add the sub-goals to the calendar on the next page.

WK 37

|   | MORNING | AFTERNOON | NIGHT |
|---|---|---|---|
| M: ___ / ___ | | | |
| T: ___ / ___ | | | |
| W: ___ / ___ | | | |
| T: ___ / ___ | | | |
| F: ___ / ___ | | | |
| S: ___ / ___ | | | |
| S: ___ / ___ | | | |

# Writing Prompt

*Each writing prompt is optional. If, for whatever reason, it does not speak to you, let it be. Who knows? It might make more sense to do the prompt later in the process.*

Every writer has their own worldview, and, one way or another, this will seep into your writing. Sometimes rather explicitly, but it can be absolutely subtle, no matter what genre you write in.

What does your writing say about your worldview? Is it in the settings you pick? The worlds you build? The themes you consciously or unconsciously apply? The characters you bring to life? The dialogue you let spill from their mouths? Grab a notebook or open a new document on your computer. Set the timer to fifteen minutes and write down your answer.

# Week 38

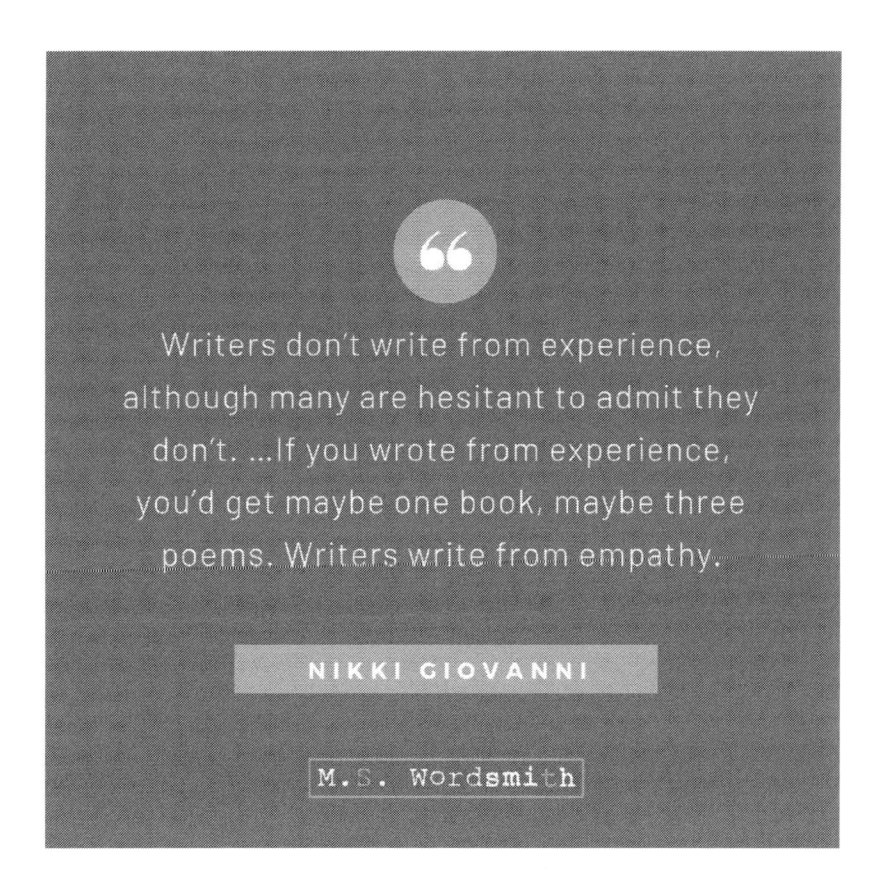

> Writers don't write from experience, although many are hesitant to admit they don't. ...If you wrote from experience, you'd get maybe one book, maybe three poems. Writers write from empathy.
>
> **NIKKI GIOVANNI**

`M.S. Wordsmith`

NINE MONTHS... YOU'RE SO CLOSE—KEEP GOING!

DATE: ...........................................................

# TRACKING

What goal(s) did you set for the past week?

Did you achieve your goal(s)?

WK 38

# Tracking

If yes, did you expect too little of yourself, or was your goal just right? If no, what prevented you from achieving it?

If you didn't reach your goals, what can you do next week to make sure you do?

If you picked an accountability partner last week, was this the right person? What worked and what didn't? Is there anything you'll want to do differently next week?

# PLANNING

What are your goals for the upcoming week?

Have another look. Are you sure this is realistic?
If not, what would be more realistic?

What can you do this week to make sure you achieve your goal(s)?

# PLANNING

What smaller pieces can you break your goal(s) up into?
Once you're sure you can't break it down anymore, add the sub-goals to the calendar on the next page.

WK 38

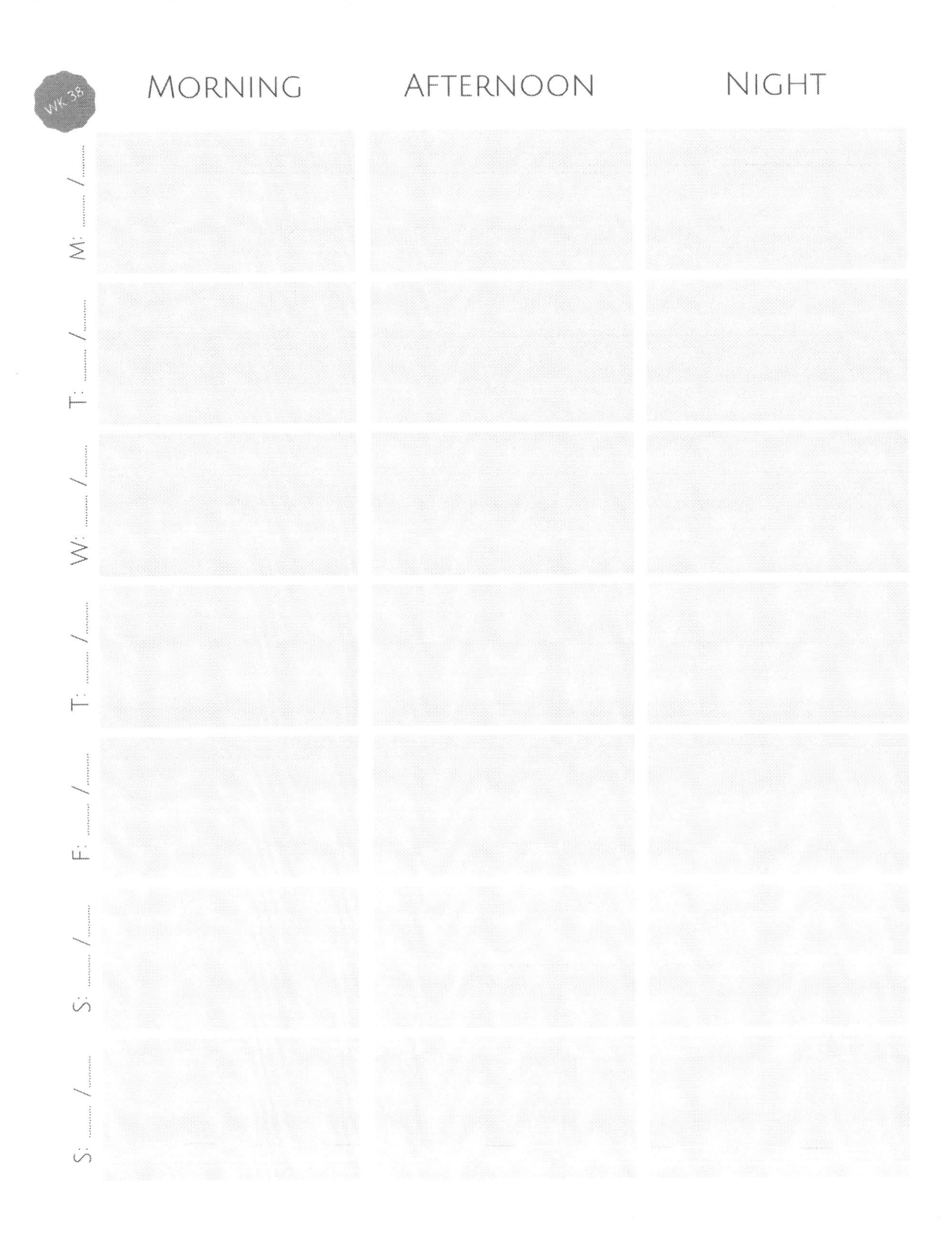

| | MORNING | AFTERNOON | NIGHT |
|---|---|---|---|
| M: __ / __ | | | |
| T: __ / __ | | | |
| W: __ / __ | | | |
| T: __ / __ | | | |
| F: __ / __ | | | |
| S: __ / __ | | | |
| S: __ / __ | | | |

# Writing Prompt

*Each writing prompt is optional. If, for whatever reason, it does not speak to you, let it be. Who knows? It might make more sense to do the prompt later in the process.*

How much of yourself do you (un)consciously pour into your characters? Do you ever write someone into existence who is nothing like you? Do you dare crawl into their skin?

Think up a character who doesn't resemble you in the slightest, whether that's because they have an entirely different profession, gender, sexuality, race/ethnicity, class, childhood trauma, and so on. Grab a notebook or open a new document on your computer. Set the timer to twenty minutes and write a scene from this person's point of view.

If you're one of those writers who find it easier to write about characters who don't mirror them in any way, try for the opposite approach. Set the timer to twenty minutes and write a scene from a character's Point of View whose life strongly resonates with your own.

# Week 39

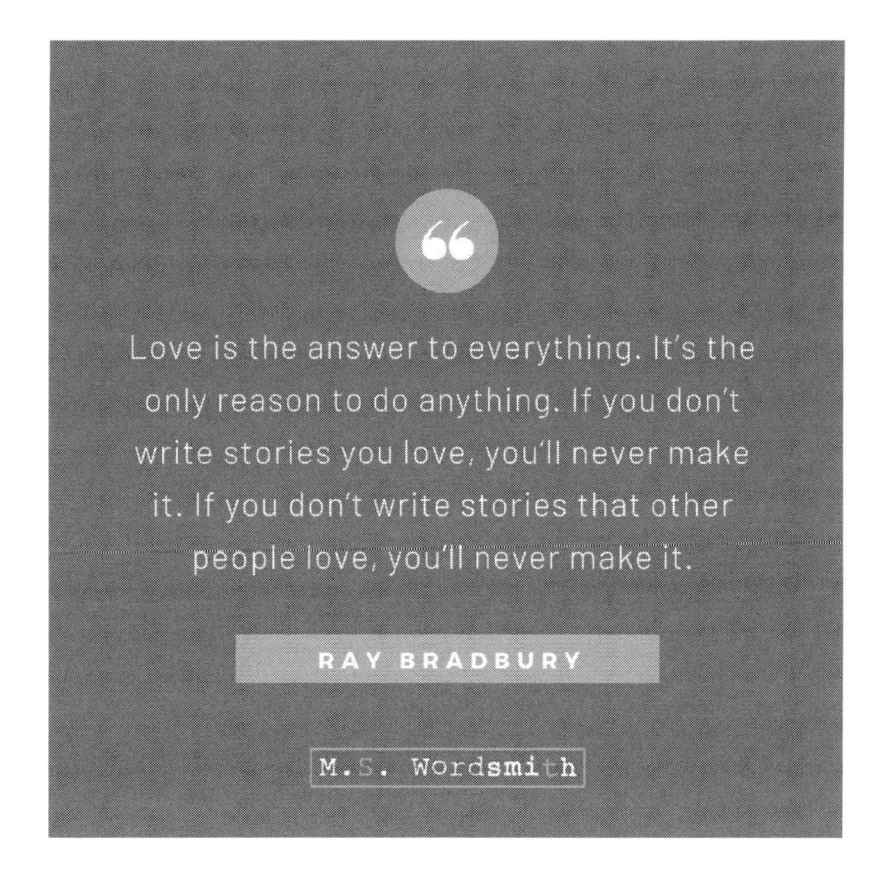

> Love is the answer to everything. It's the only reason to do anything. If you don't write stories you love, you'll never make it. If you don't write stories that other people love, you'll never make it.
>
> **RAY BRADBURY**

M.S. Wordsmith

DATE: ...........................................................................

# TRACKING

What goal(s) did you set for the past week?

Did you achieve your goal(s)?

WK 39

# Tracking

If yes, did you expect too little of yourself, or was your goal just right? If no, what prevented you from achieving it?

If you didn't reach your goals, what can you do next week to make sure you do?

If you picked an accountability partner last week, was this the right person? What worked and what didn't? Is there anything you'll want to do differently next week?

WK 39

# PLANNING

What are your goals for the upcoming week?

Have another look. Are you sure this is realistic?
If not, what would be more realistic?

What can you do this week to make sure you achieve your goal(s)?

# PLANNING

What smaller pieces can you break your goal(s) up into?
Once you're sure you can't break it down anymore, add the sub-goals to the calendar on the next page.

WK 39

| | MORNING | AFTERNOON | NIGHT |
|---|---|---|---|
| M: / | | | |
| T: / | | | |
| W: / | | | |
| T: / | | | |
| F: / | | | |
| S: / | | | |
| S: / | | | |

# WRITING PROMPT

*Each writing prompt is optional. If, for whatever reason, it does not speak to you, let it be. Who knows? It might make more sense to do the prompt later in the process.*

Grab a notebook or open a new document on your computer. Set the timer to twenty minutes and draw up a list of all the themes you love to explore in your writing, no matter how dark or twisted or cheesy or steamy.

Once you're done, set the timer again. For each item on the list, write down why other people would love to read what you have to say about any of these items.

Nine months have passed!

Did you think you'd make it this far?

# How are you going to celebrate?

Write it down, then go do it!

# WEEK 40

> Finish the damn book. Nothing else matters. Stop second-guessing yourself and write it through to the end. You don't know what you have until you've finished it. You don't know how to fix it until it's all down on the page.
>
> **LAUREN BEUKES**

M.S. Wordsmith

DATE: ...........................................

# CLARITY

During Week One, you wrote down why you were first called to write. Over the past three months, have you been able to reconnect to that calling? Take a moment to reflect.

Over the past three months, have you been able to reconnect to how writing used to make you feel? There are no right or wrong answers here. Like the calling, your feelings about writing might have shifted. Take a moment to reflect on this as well.

# CLARITY

Looking back over the past three months, how did the act of writing make you feel? How did you feel right before you started, during, and once you were done?

Are you dealing with the same struggles and roadblocks you identified when we started this journey, or have they changed? If they have, what are you currently struggling with?

# CLARITY

For each struggle and roadblock you are (still) dealing with, can you determine which are internal or external? Even if your list hasn't changed, still reflect on this. Something might very well have shifted in the meantime.

# CLARITY

For each struggle and roadblock, what do you think you need to overcome it? If you're still dealing with the same struggle(s) or roadblock(s), this doesn't mean you didn't make any progress. This is where you get to reflect and determine whether you did.

# REFLECTING

Let's take a moment to reflect. When looking back on the past three months, what are you most grateful for?

What are the most significant lessons you have learned about yourself and your writing?

Did you achieve your 3-month goal(s)? If yes, (how) did you celebrate? If not, what steps could you take from this week onwards to ensure you reach your next 3-month goal(s)?

WK 40

# GOALS

*Do these goals still hold true or is it time to adjust them?*

Where do you want to be in the next fifty-two weeks? How are you going to celebrate?

In nine months? How are you going to celebrate?

In six months? How are you going to celebrate?

In three months? How are you going to celebrate?

# Tracking

What goal(s) did you set for the past week?

Did you achieve your goal(s)?

WK 40

# TRACKING

If yes, did you expect too little of yourself, or was your goal just right? If no, what prevented you from achieving it?

If you didn't reach your goals, what can you do next week to make sure you do?

If you picked an accountability partner last week, was this the right person? What worked and what didn't? Is there anything you'll want to do differently next week?

# PLANNING

What are your goals for the upcoming week?

Have another look. Are you sure this is realistic?
If not, what would be more realistic?

What can you do this week to make sure you achieve your goal(s)?

WK 40

# Planning

What smaller pieces can you break your goal(s) up into?
Once you're sure you can't break it down anymore, add the sub-goals to the calendar on the next page.

|  | MORNING | AFTERNOON | NIGHT |
|---|---|---|---|
| WK 40 | | | |
| M: / | | | |
| T: / | | | |
| W: / | | | |
| T: / | | | |
| F: / | | | |
| S: / | | | |
| S: / | | | |

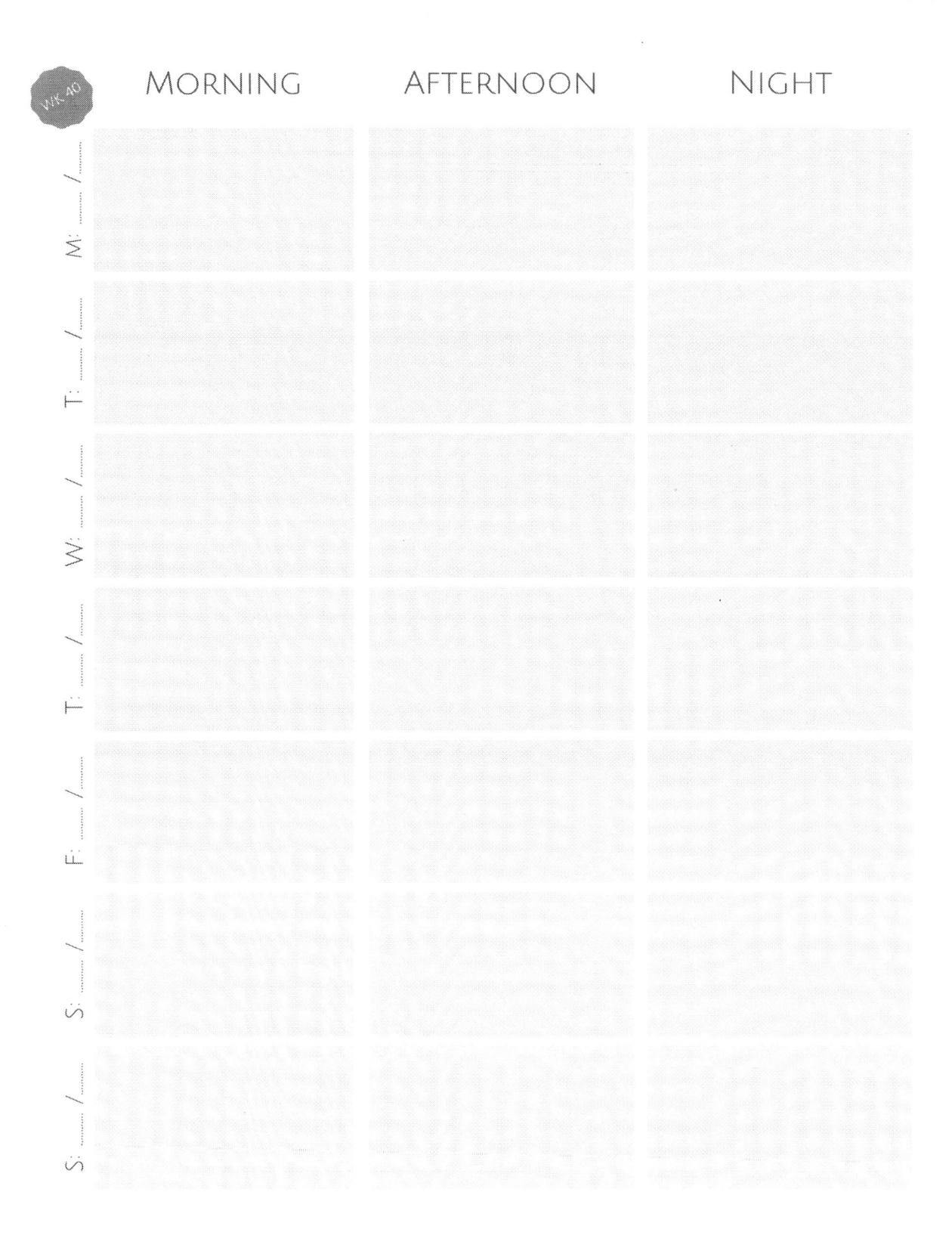

# Writing Prompt

*Each writing prompt is optional. If, for whatever reason, it does not speak to you, let it be. Who knows? It might make more sense to do the prompt later in the process.*

Who are you writing for? Yourself? Your great-great-grandmother who never had the chance to become a writer? That inspiring elementary school teacher who never stopped believing in you? One of your parents, or both?

Grab a notebook or open a new document on your computer. Set the timer to twenty minutes and ask yourself who you want to reach 'The End' for. Whoever it is, write them a letter—even if it's you!—and explain to them why you have what it takes to reach that finish line.

# WEEK 41

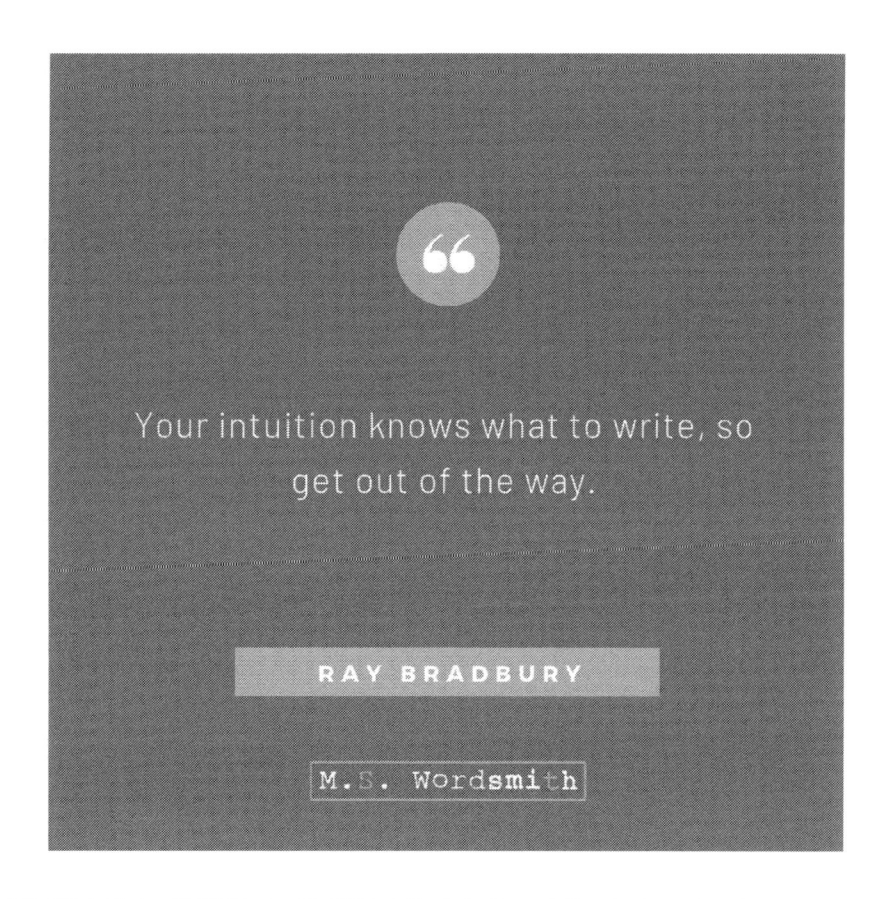

> Your intuition knows what to write, so get out of the way.
>
> **RAY BRADBURY**

M.S. Wordsmith

IF THIS WEEK'S WRITING PROMPT IS PARTICULARLY CHALLENGING, I HAVE AN EXTRA EXERCISE THAT COULD BE HELPFUL. YOU CAN FIND ME AT MARIELLE@MSWORDSMITH.NL

DATE: _____

# TRACKING

What goal(s) did you set for the past week?

Did you achieve your goal(s)?

WK 41

# Tracking

If yes, did you expect too little of yourself, or was your goal just right? If no, what prevented you from achieving it?

If you didn't reach your goals, what can you do next week to make sure you do?

If you picked an accountability partner last week, was this the right person? What worked and what didn't? Is there anything you'll want to do differently next week?

# PLANNING

What are your goals for the upcoming week?

Have another look. Are you sure this is realistic?
If not, what would be more realistic?

What can you do this week to make sure you achieve your goal(s)?

WK 41

# PLANNING

What smaller pieces can you break your goal(s) up into?
Once you're sure you can't break it down anymore, add the sub-goals to the calendar on the next page.

WK 41

WK 41

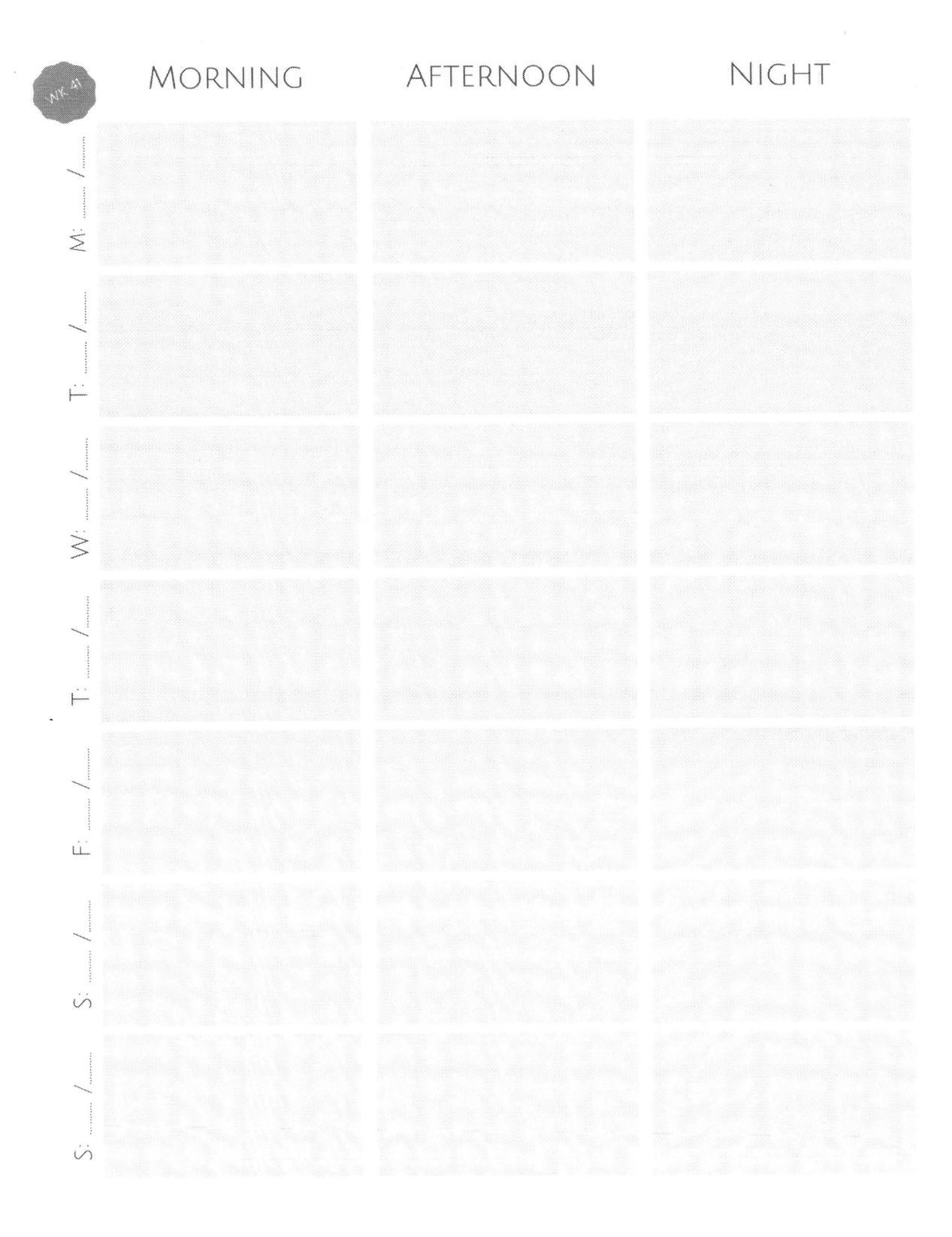

|  | MORNING | AFTERNOON | NIGHT |
|---|---|---|---|
| M: __/__ |  |  |  |
| T: __/__ |  |  |  |
| W: __/__ |  |  |  |
| T: __/__ |  |  |  |
| F: __/__ |  |  |  |
| S: __/__ |  |  |  |
| S: __/__ |  |  |  |

# Writing Prompt

*Each writing prompt is optional. If, for whatever reason, it does not speak to you, let it be. Who knows? It might make more sense to do the prompt later in the process.*

How often does your head get in the way when you're writing?

This week, whenever you find your thoughts disrupting your writing process, pause and take note. What thoughts were you having? You don't have to engage with them just yet; jot them down and try to get back to writing. If that doesn't work, take a small break, even if it's just to grab a glass of water.

At the end of the week, look at the thoughts you've collected. Do you notice anything in particular? Does it tell you anything about your thought processes while you're writing, or how your head tries to get in the way of your intuition? Did it help to scribble the thoughts down before you continued writing?

# Week 42

> A writer is a writer not because she writes well and easily, because she has amazing talent, or because everything she does is golden. A writer is a writer because, even when there is no hope, even when nothing you do shows any sign of promise, you keep writing anyway.
>
> **JUNOT DIAZ**

M.S. Wordsmith

DATE: ........................................

# Tracking

What goal(s) did you set for the past week?

Did you achieve your goal(s)?

WK 42

# Tracking

If yes, did you expect too little of yourself, or was your goal just right? If no, what prevented you from achieving it?

If you didn't reach your goals, what can you do next week to make sure you do?

If you picked an accountability partner last week, was this the right person? What worked and what didn't? Is there anything you'll want to do differently next week?

# PLANNING

What are your goals for the upcoming week?

Have another look. Are you sure this is realistic?
If not, what would be more realistic?

What can you do this week to make sure you achieve your goal(s)?

WK 42

# Planning

What smaller pieces can you break your goal(s) up into?
Once you're sure you can't break it down anymore, add the sub-goals to the calendar on the next page.

## WK 42

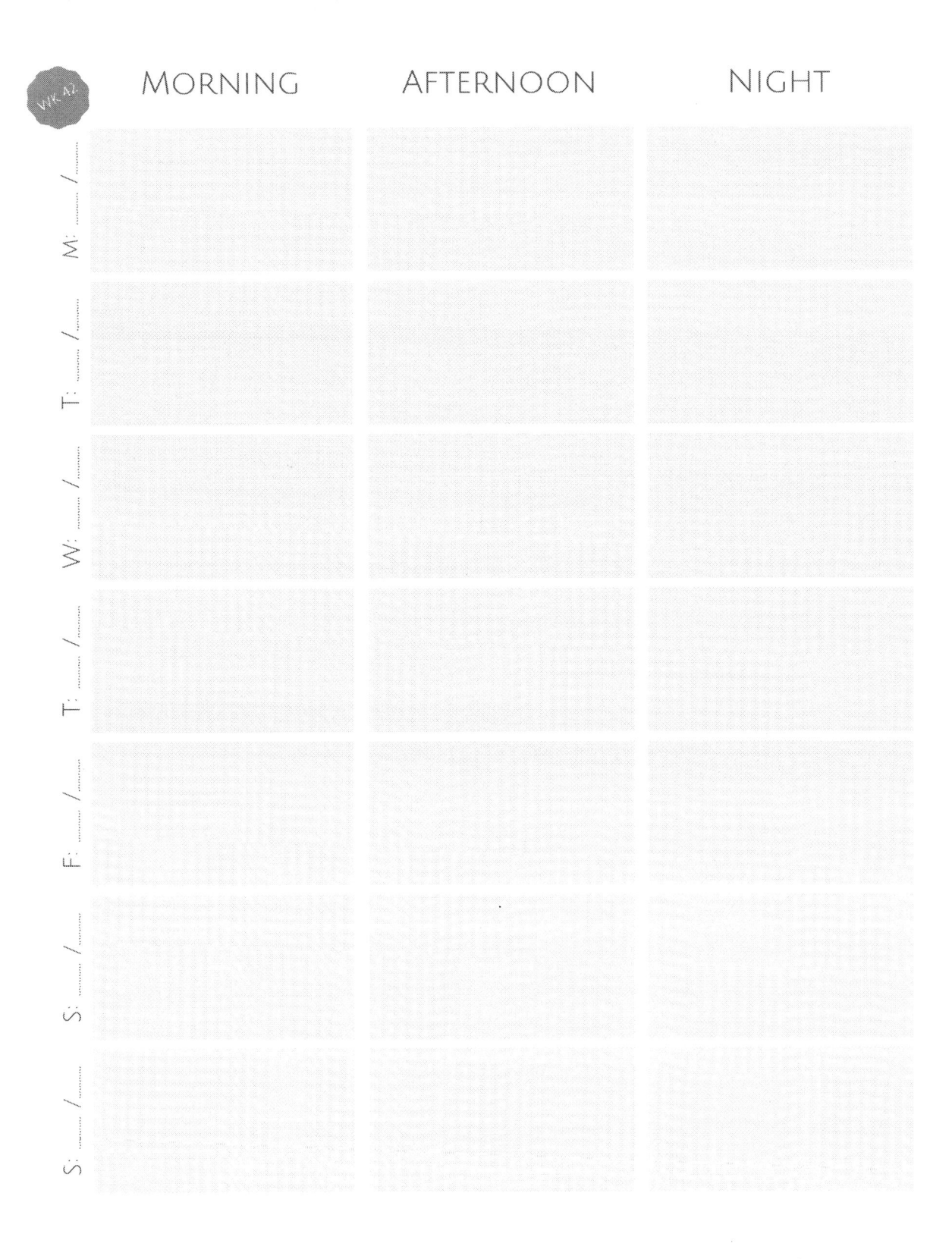

|  | MORNING | AFTERNOON | NIGHT |
|---|---|---|---|
| M: __ / __ | | | |
| T: __ / __ | | | |
| W: __ / __ | | | |
| T: __ / __ | | | |
| F: __ / __ | | | |
| S: __ / __ | | | |
| S: __ / __ | | | |

# WRITING PROMPT

*Each writing prompt is optional. If, for whatever reason, it does not speak to you, let it be. Who knows? It might make more sense to do the prompt later in the process.*

How often have you lost hope, only to return to your writing weeks, months, years (or even decades!) later? What made you come back?

Grab a notebook or open a new document on your computer. Set the timer to twenty minutes and think back to all those times you nearly gave up. You came back for a reason, but do you know what that reason is? Can you distil it, summarise it in one or two simple phrases?

If not, return to this exercise later. It might take a while to define what it is exactly that made you have another go at it. If yes, write the words down on a separate piece of paper and put it somewhere you see it every day.

# WEEK 43

> Done is better than perfect.
>
> **SHERYL SANDBERG**
>
> M.S. Wordsmith

DATE: ...................................................

# TRACKING

What goal(s) did you set for the past week?

Did you achieve your goal(s)?

WK 43

# TRACKING

If yes, did you expect too little of yourself, or was your goal just right? If no, what prevented you from achieving it?

If you didn't reach your goals, what can you do next week to make sure you do?

If you picked an accountability partner last week, was this the right person? What worked and what didn't? Is there anything you'll want to do differently next week?

# PLANNING

What are your goals for the upcoming week?

Have another look. Are you sure this is realistic?
If not, what would be more realistic?

What can you do this week to make sure you achieve your goal(s)?

# PLANNING

What smaller pieces can you break your goal(s) up into?
Once you're sure you can't break it down anymore, add the sub-goals to the calendar on the next page.

WK 43

WK 43

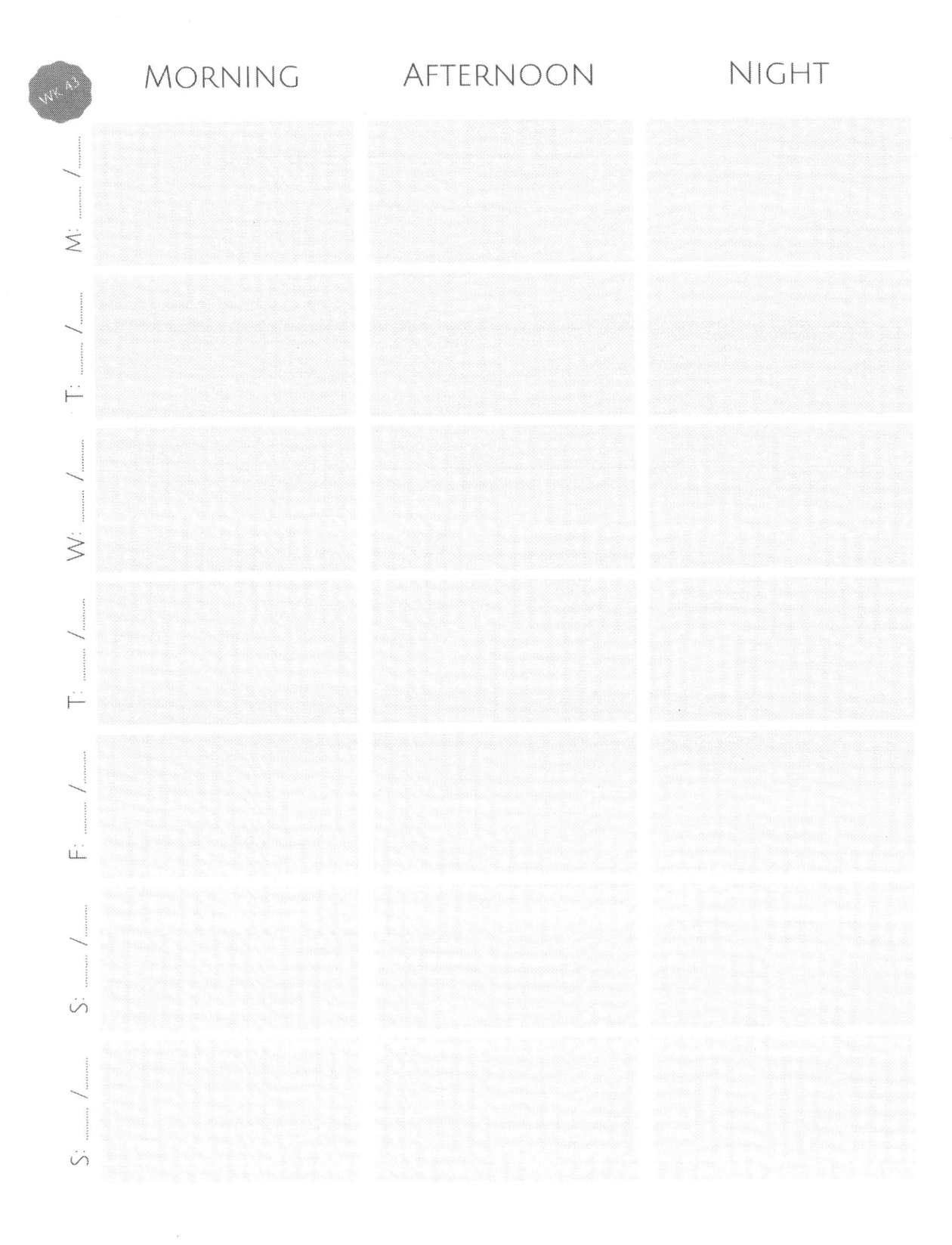

| | MORNING | AFTERNOON | NIGHT |
|---|---|---|---|
| M: __/__ | | | |
| T: __/__ | | | |
| W: __/__ | | | |
| T: __/__ | | | |
| F: __/__ | | | |
| S: __/__ | | | |
| S: __/__ | | | |

# Writing Prompt

*Each writing prompt is optional. If, for whatever reason, it does not speak to you, let it be. Who knows? It might make more sense to do the prompt later in the process.*

Are you a perfectionist or does it come naturally to you to finish one story and move on to the next?

Each time you finish a piece, ask yourself whether it's done. Really sit with that question for a bit.

If you have trouble deciding this for yourself, ask for opinions of the people you trust. Critical readers, writing buddies, anyone who will provide constructive criticism. Together, can you decide that it's time to move on to your next adventure?

# WEEK 44

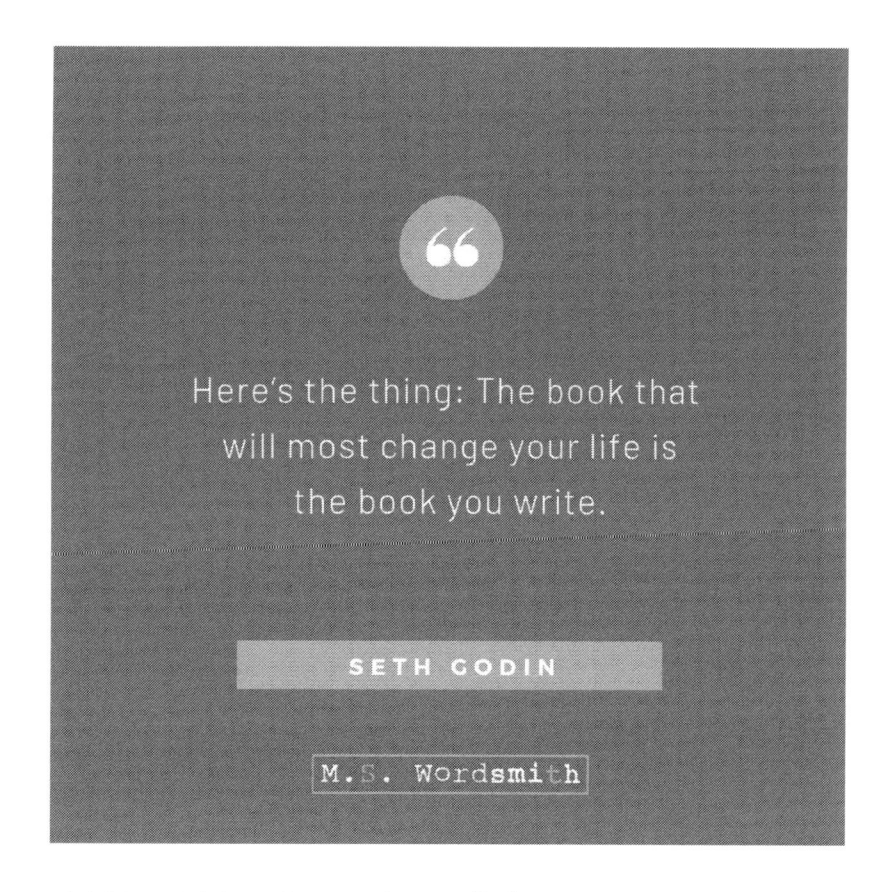

> Here's the thing: The book that will most change your life is the book you write.
>
> **SETH GODIN**
>
> M.S. Wordsmith

HOW ARE YOU DOING? BETTER THAN EVER OR BARELY HANGING IN THERE?

DATE: ........................................................

# Tracking

What goal(s) did you set for the past week?

Did you achieve your goal(s)?

WK 44

# TRACKING

If yes, did you expect too little of yourself, or was your goal just right? If no, what prevented you from achieving it?

If you didn't reach your goals, what can you do next week to make sure you do?

If you picked an accountability partner last week, was this the right person? What worked and what didn't? Is there anything you'll want to do differently next week?

# PLANNING

What are your goals for the upcoming week?

Have another look. Are you sure this is realistic?
If not, what would be more realistic?

What can you do this week to make sure you achieve your goal(s)?

WK 44

# PLANNING

What smaller pieces can you break your goal(s) up into?
Once you're sure you can't break it down anymore, add the sub-goals to the calendar on the next page.

| | Morning | Afternoon | Night |
|---|---|---|---|
| **Wk 44** | | | |
| M: / | | | |
| T: / | | | |
| W: / | | | |
| T: / | | | |
| F: / | | | |
| S: / | | | |
| S: / | | | |

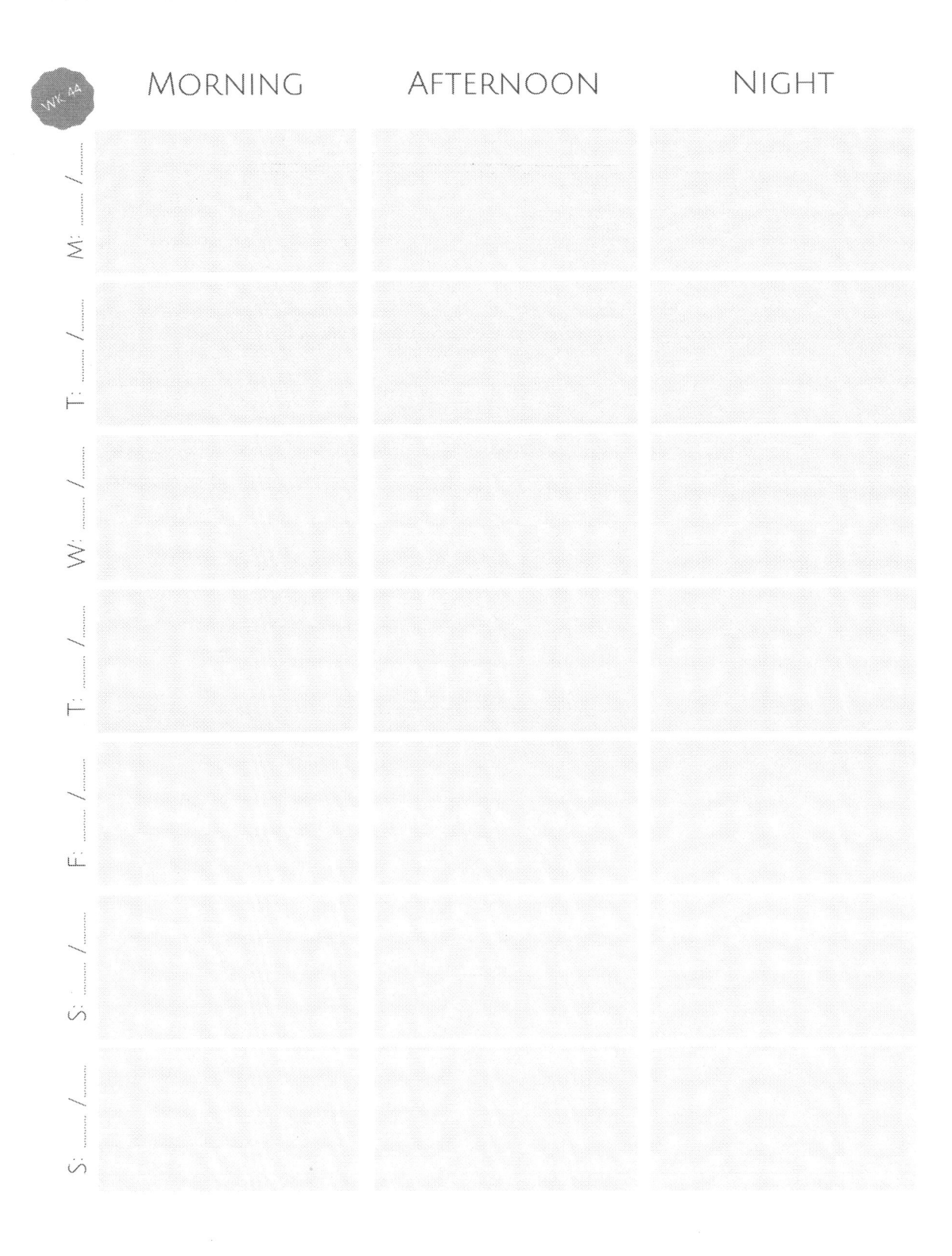

# WRITING PROMPT

*Each writing prompt is optional. If, for whatever reason, it does not speak to you, let it be. Who knows? It might make more sense to do the prompt later in the process.*

How will this story you're writing change your life?

Grab a notebook or open a new document on your computer. Set the timer to 20 minutes and write down exactly how it will. What will it bring you? What will it make you discover about life? Yourself? How will it make you grow? How will it allow for you to connect to others?

# WEEK 45

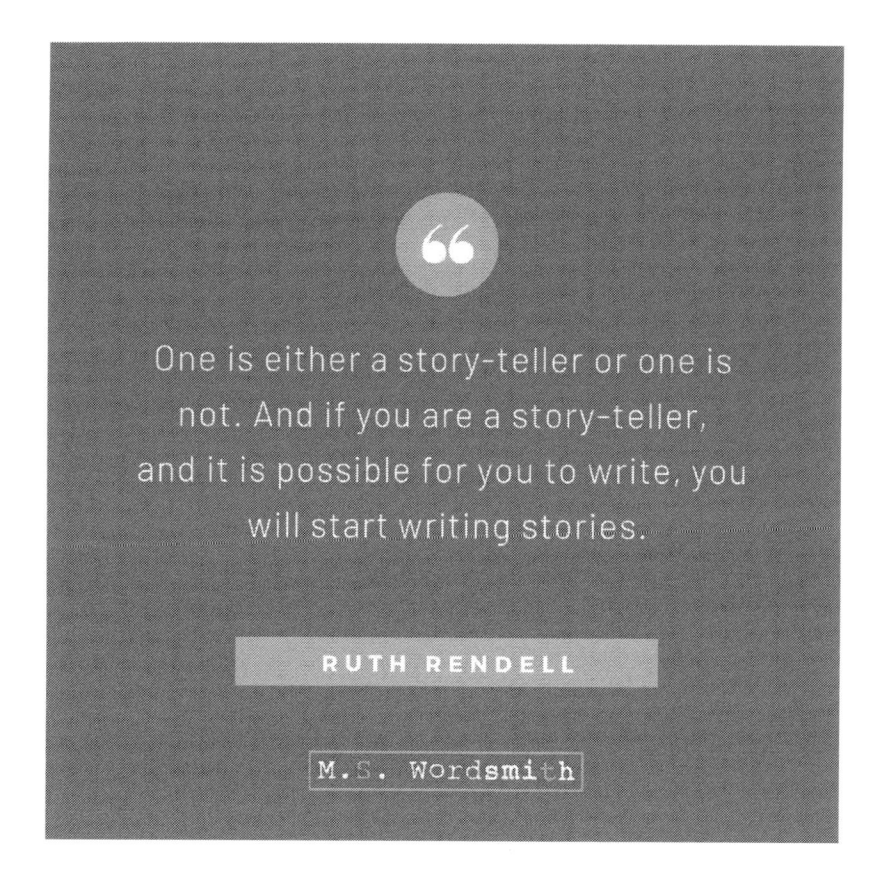

> One is either a story-teller or one is not. And if you are a story-teller, and it is possible for you to write, you will start writing stories.
>
> **RUTH RENDELL**
>
> M.S. Wordsmith

DATE: _____

# TRACKING

What goal(s) did you set for the past week?

Did you achieve your goal(s)?

WK 45

# Tracking

If yes, did you expect too little of yourself, or was your goal just right? If no, what prevented you from achieving it?

If you didn't reach your goals, what can you do next week to make sure you do?

If you picked an accountability partner last week, was this the right person? What worked and what didn't? Is there anything you'll want to do differently next week?

# PLANNING

What are your goals for the upcoming week?

Have another look. Are you sure this is realistic?
If not, what would be more realistic?

What can you do this week to make sure you achieve your goal(s)?

# Planning

What smaller pieces can you break your goal(s) up into?
Once you're sure you can't break it down anymore, add the sub-goals to the calendar on the next page.

WK 45

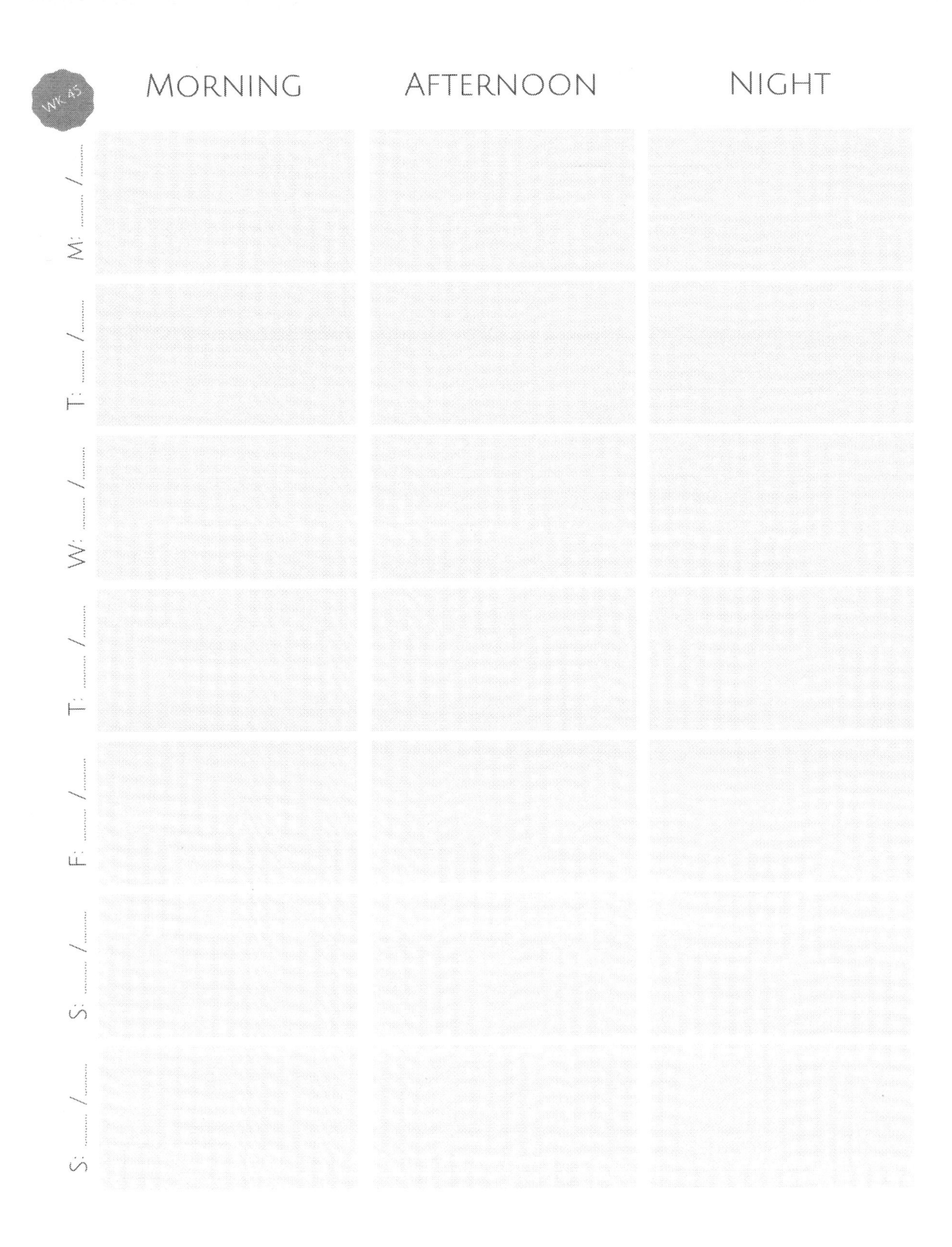

|  | MORNING | AFTERNOON | NIGHT |
|---|---|---|---|
| M: __ / __ | | | |
| T: __ / __ | | | |
| W: __ / __ | | | |
| T: __ / __ | | | |
| F: __ / __ | | | |
| S: __ / __ | | | |
| S: __ / __ | | | |

# WRITING PROMPT

*Each writing prompt is optional. If, for whatever reason, it does not speak to you, let it be. Who knows? It might make more sense to do the prompt later in the process.*

Having the uncontrollable need to write can easily become something that sets you apart from everyone else around you. This is one of the reasons why belonging to a community is vital. Embracing that you're a storyteller will become so much easier when you surround yourself with other storytellers.

Are you part of a writing community, online or offline? If you already are, take a good look at this particular community and ask yourself whether it's giving you what you need. If you aren't yet, search for at least one new community this week. Perhaps there are some local groups you can check out? If you prefer to connect online, just open a browser or Facebook and explore to your heart's content. With so many groups out there, there will be one that speaks to you.

# Week 46

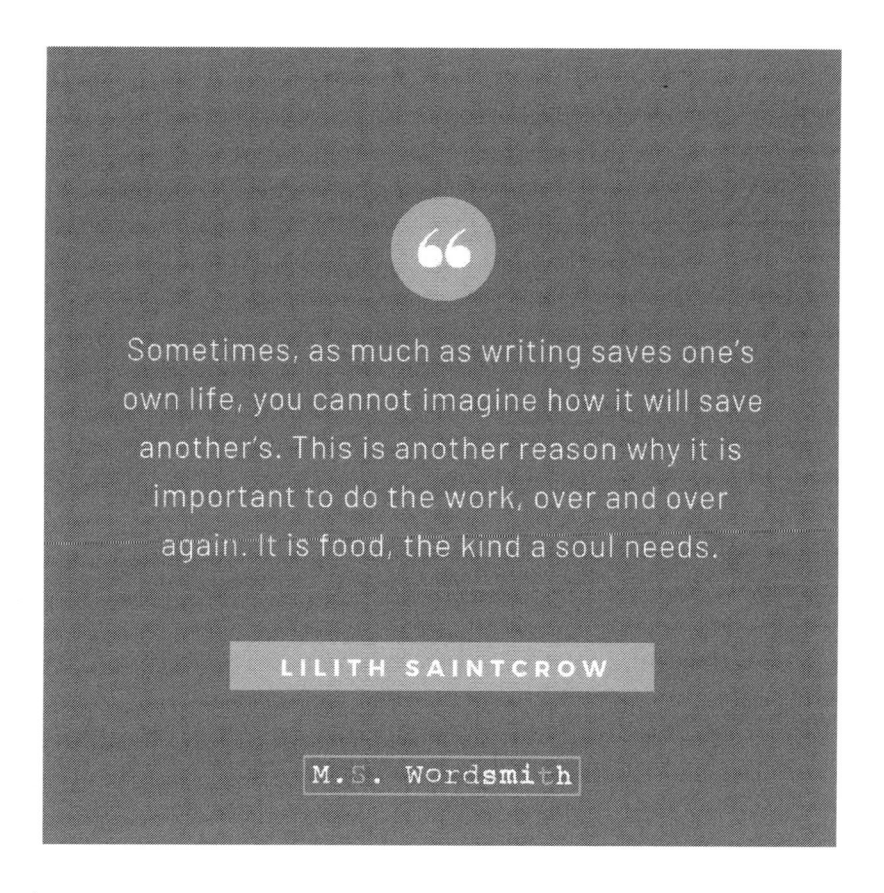

> Sometimes, as much as writing saves one's own life, you cannot imagine how it will save another's. This is another reason why it is important to do the work, over and over again. It is food, the kind a soul needs.
>
> **LILITH SAINTCROW**
>
> M.S. Wordsmith

I CAN ALMOST SEE THE FINISH LINE! CAN YOU BELIEVE YOU'RE STILL HERE, DOING THIS?

DATE: _____

# TRACKING

What goal(s) did you set for the past week?

Did you achieve your goal(s)?

WK 46

# Tracking

If yes, did you expect too little of yourself, or was your goal just right? If no, what prevented you from achieving it?

If you didn't reach your goals, what can you do next week to make sure you do?

If you picked an accountability partner last week, was this the right person? What worked and what didn't? Is there anything you'll want to do differently next week?

# PLANNING

What are your goals for the upcoming week?

Have another look. Are you sure this is realistic?
If not, what would be more realistic?

What can you do this week to make sure you achieve your goal(s)?

# PLANNING

What smaller pieces can you break your goal(s) up into?
Once you're sure you can't break it down anymore, add the sub-goals to the calendar on the next page.

WK 46

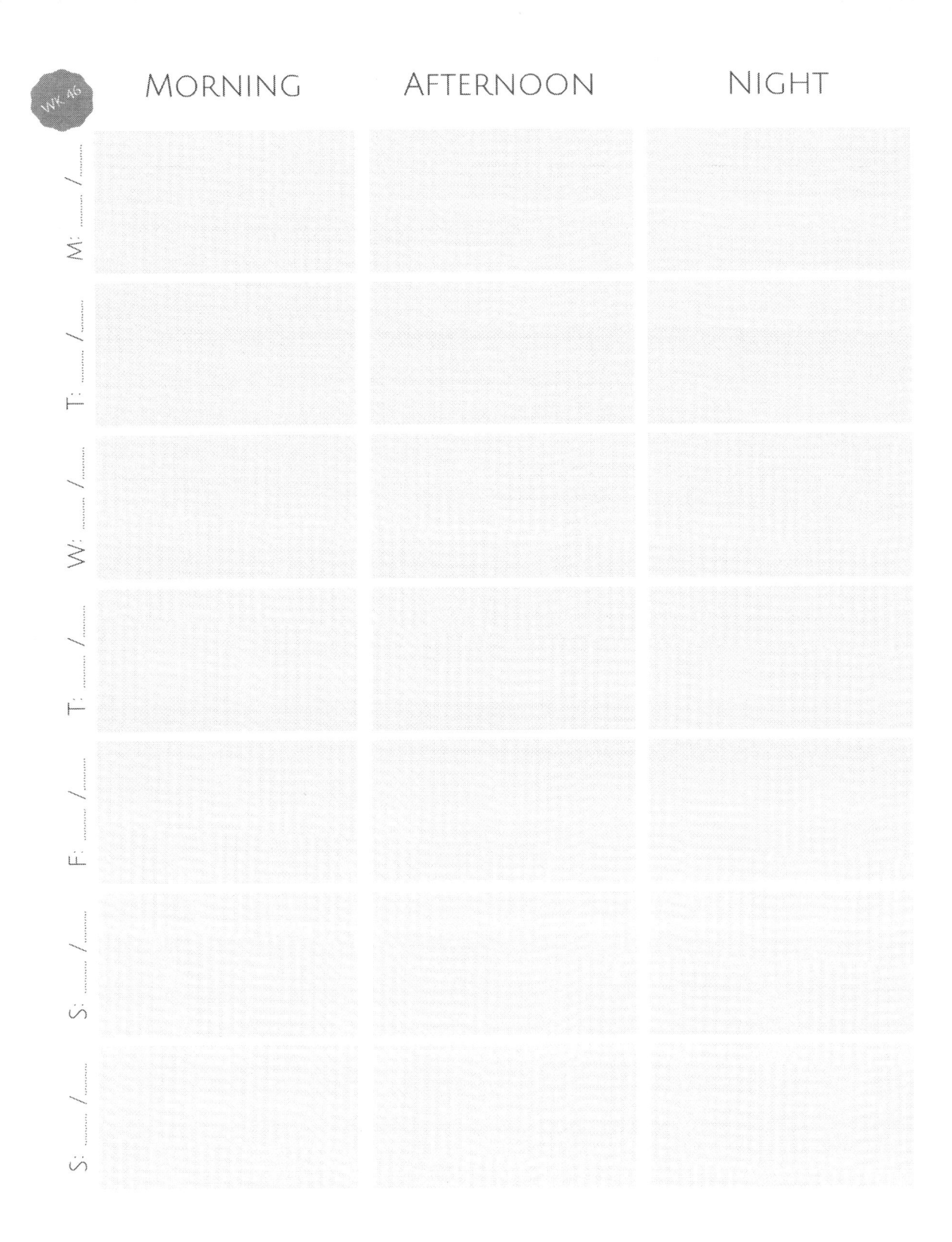

|   | MORNING | AFTERNOON | NIGHT |
|---|---|---|---|
| M: / |  |  |  |
| T: / |  |  |  |
| W: / |  |  |  |
| T: / |  |  |  |
| F: / |  |  |  |
| S: / |  |  |  |
| S: / |  |  |  |

# WRITING PROMPT

*Each writing prompt is optional. If, for whatever reason, it does not speak to you, let it be. Who knows? It might make more sense to do the prompt later in the process.*

It doesn't matter what you write; somewhere, someone is waiting for your story to come out.

What if this person, after reading your book, were to send you a letter or email? Grab a notebook or open a new document on your computer. Set the timer to twenty minutes and write down your response to this imaginary (for now!) piece of correspondence.

If you already received your first fanmail, take this moment to reflect on how it made you feel. What did you do after reading it?

# Week 47

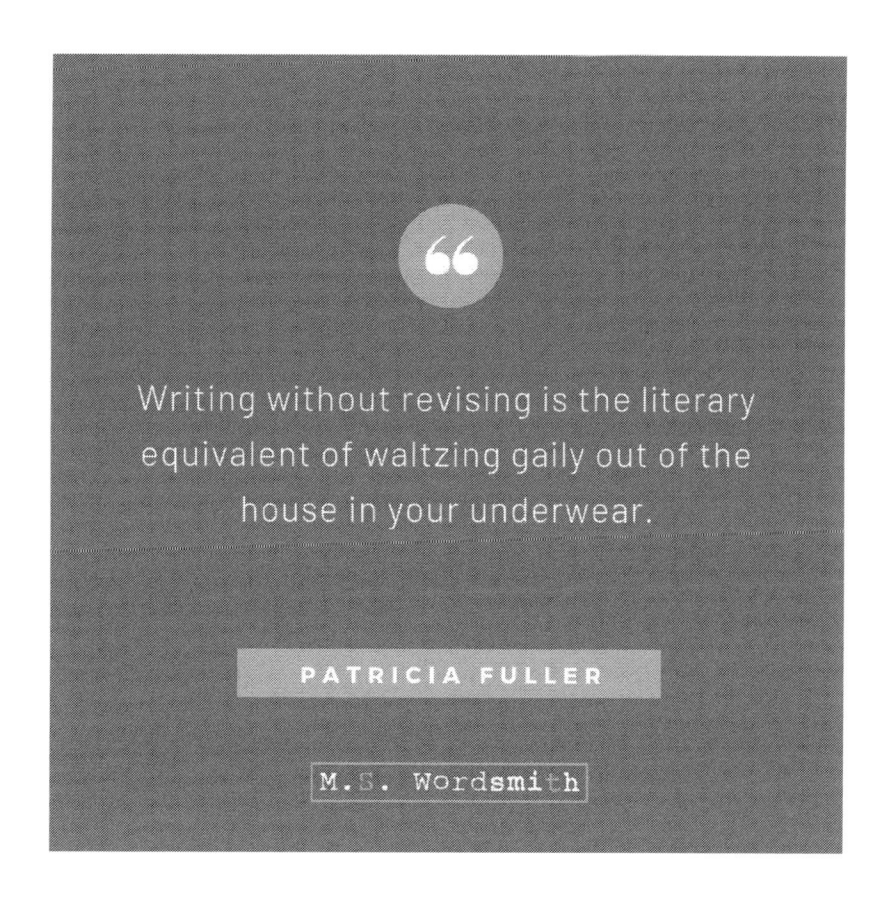

> Writing without revising is the literary equivalent of waltzing gaily out of the house in your underwear.
>
> **PATRICIA FULLER**
>
> M.S. Wordsmith

DATE: _____

# Tracking

What goal(s) did you set for the past week?

Did you achieve your goal(s)?

# Tracking

If yes, did you expect too little of yourself, or was your goal just right? If no, what prevented you from achieving it?

If you didn't reach your goals, what can you do next week to make sure you do?

If you picked an accountability partner last week, was this the right person? What worked and what didn't? Is there anything you'll want to do differently next week?

# PLANNING

What are your goals for the upcoming week?

Have another look. Are you sure this is realistic?
If not, what would be more realistic?

What can you do this week to make sure you achieve your goal(s)?

# Planning

What smaller pieces can you break your goal(s) up into?
Once you're sure you can't break it down anymore, add the sub-goals to the calendar on the next page.

WK 47

| | MORNING | AFTERNOON | NIGHT |
|---|---|---|---|
| M: __ / __ | | | |
| T: __ / __ | | | |
| W: __ / __ | | | |
| T: __ / __ | | | |
| F: __ / __ | | | |
| S: __ / __ | | | |
| S: __ / __ | | | |

# WRITING PROMPT

*Each writing prompt is optional. If, for whatever reason, it does not speak to you, let it be. Who knows? It might make more sense to do the prompt later in the process.*

For how long do you usually take a break from your writing before you start revising? Every author has their own method, but it's always good to take any kind of break.

Go online and search for advice on how to take a break from your Work in Progress. Whose advice resonates most with you? The next time you finish a piece, take their advice to heart and see whether it works for you. If not, try someone else's system or adjust to your personal needs and wishes.

# WEEK 48

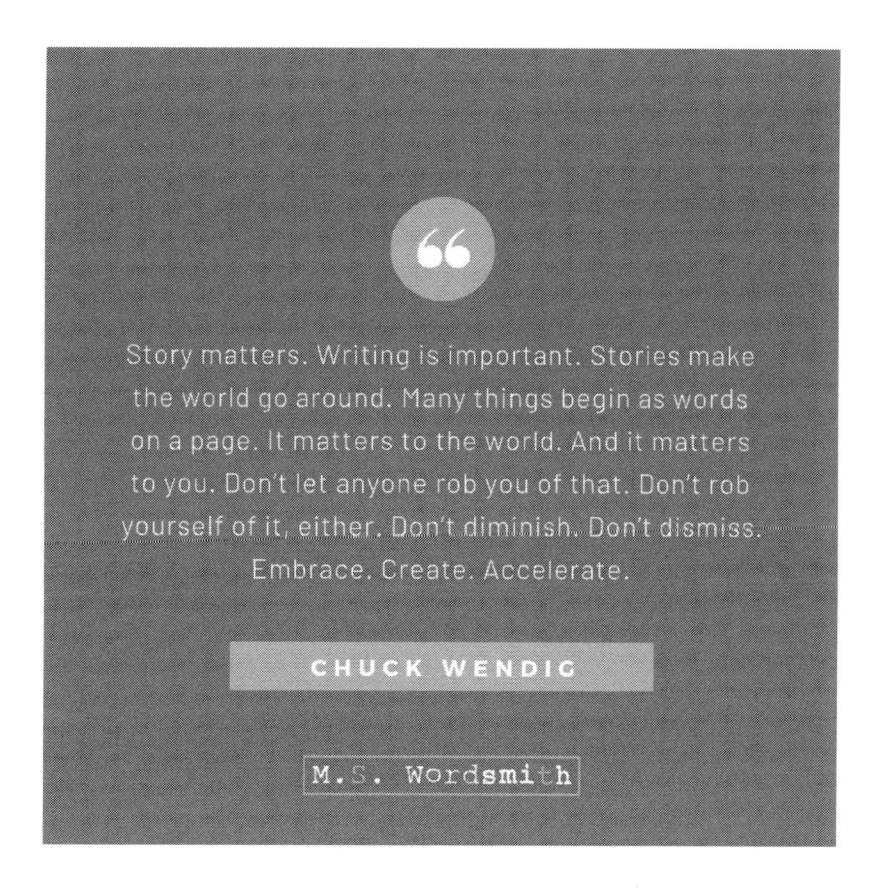

> Story matters. Writing is important. Stories make the world go around. Many things begin as words on a page. It matters to the world. And it matters to you. Don't let anyone rob you of that. Don't rob yourself of it, either. Don't diminish. Don't dismiss. Embrace. Create. Accelerate.
>
> **CHUCK WENDIG**

M.S. Wordsmith

YOU CAN DO THIS!

DATE: _____

# TRACKING

What goal(s) did you set for the past week?

Did you achieve your goal(s)?

WK 48

# Tracking

If yes, did you expect too little of yourself, or was your goal just right? If no, what prevented you from achieving it?

If you didn't reach your goals, what can you do next week to make sure you do?

If you picked an accountability partner last week, was this the right person? What worked and what didn't? Is there anything you'll want to do differently next week?

# PLANNING

What are your goals for the upcoming week?

Have another look. Are you sure this is realistic?
If not, what would be more realistic?

What can you do this week to make sure you achieve your goal(s)?

WK 48

# Planning

What smaller pieces can you break your goal(s) up into?
Once you're sure you can't break it down anymore, add the sub-goals to the calendar on the next page.

*WK 48*

**WK. 48**

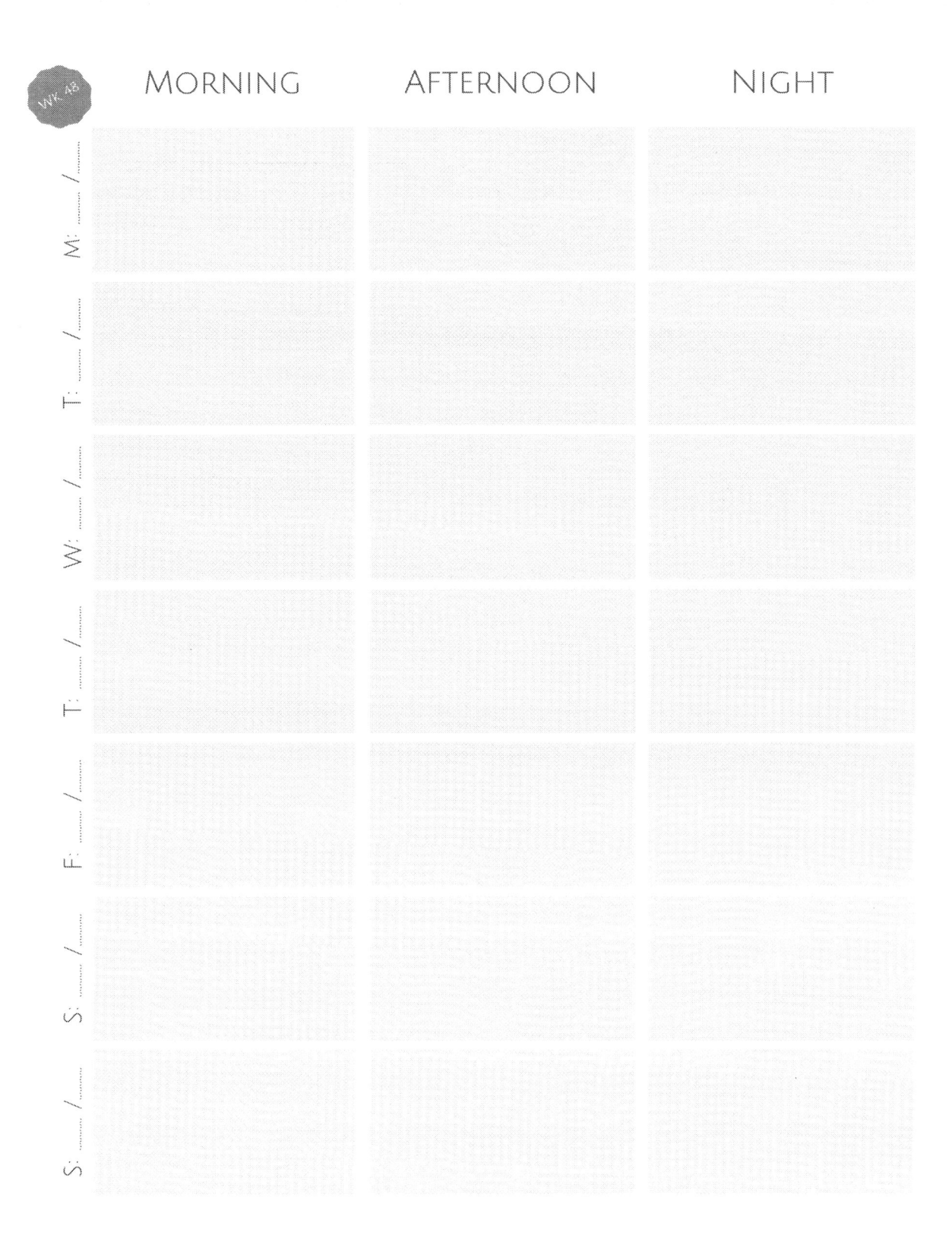

|  | MORNING | AFTERNOON | NIGHT |
|---|---|---|---|
| M: __/__ | | | |
| T: __/__ | | | |
| W: __/__ | | | |
| T: __/__ | | | |
| F: __/__ | | | |
| S: __/__ | | | |
| S: __/__ | | | |

# WRITING PROMPT

*Each writing prompt is optional. If, for whatever reason, it does not speak to you, let it be. Who knows? It might make more sense to do the prompt later in the process.*

Do the people you care about know that you write? Do you call yourself a writer, for example when you introduce yourself to new people?

If yes, how do people usually respond when you claim that title, and how did that make you feel? If not (or not always), what is keeping you from claiming it?

Grab a notebook or open a new document on your computer. Set the timer to twenty minutes and write down your answer.

# WEEK 49

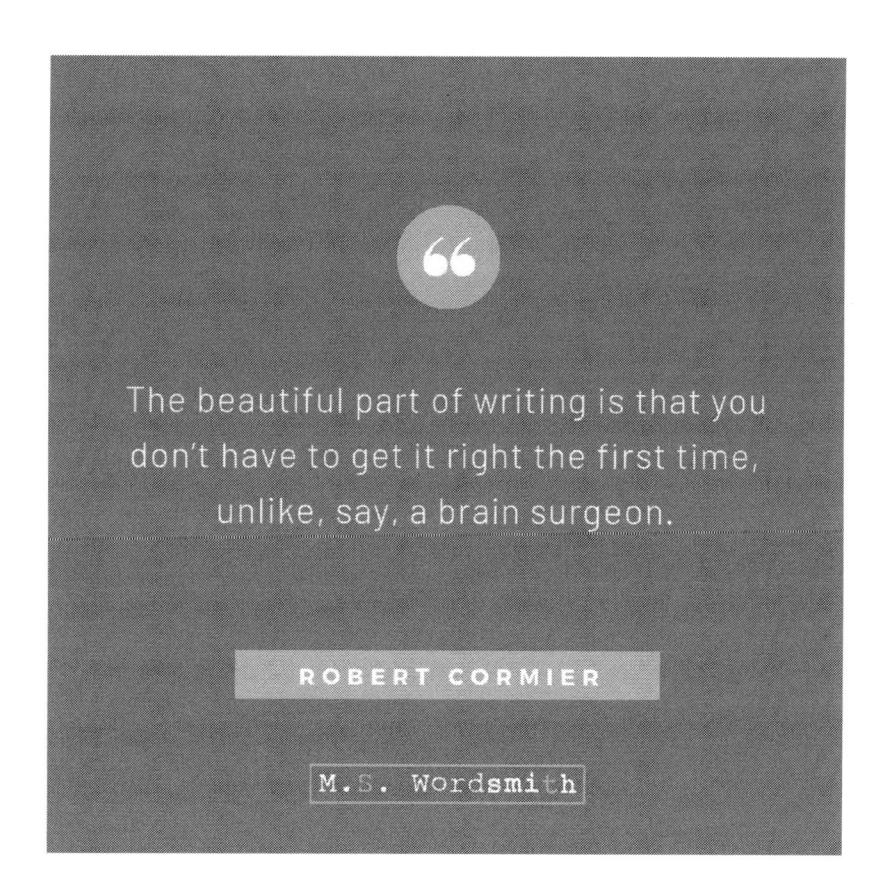

> The beautiful part of writing is that you don't have to get it right the first time, unlike, say, a brain surgeon.
>
> **ROBERT CORMIER**
>
> M.S. Wordsmith

DATE: ............................................................

# TRACKING

What goal(s) did you set for the past week?

Did you achieve your goal(s)?

WK 49

# Tracking

If yes, did you expect too little of yourself, or was your goal just right? If no, what prevented you from achieving it?

If you didn't reach your goals, what can you do next week to make sure you do?

If you picked an accountability partner last week, was this the right person? What worked and what didn't? Is there anything you'll want to do differently next week?

# PLANNING

What are your goals for the upcoming week?

Have another look. Are you sure this is realistic?
If not, what would be more realistic?

What can you do this week to make sure you achieve your goal(s)?

# PLANNING

What smaller pieces can you break your goal(s) up into?
Once you're sure you can't break it down anymore, add the sub-goals to the calendar on the next page.

WK 49

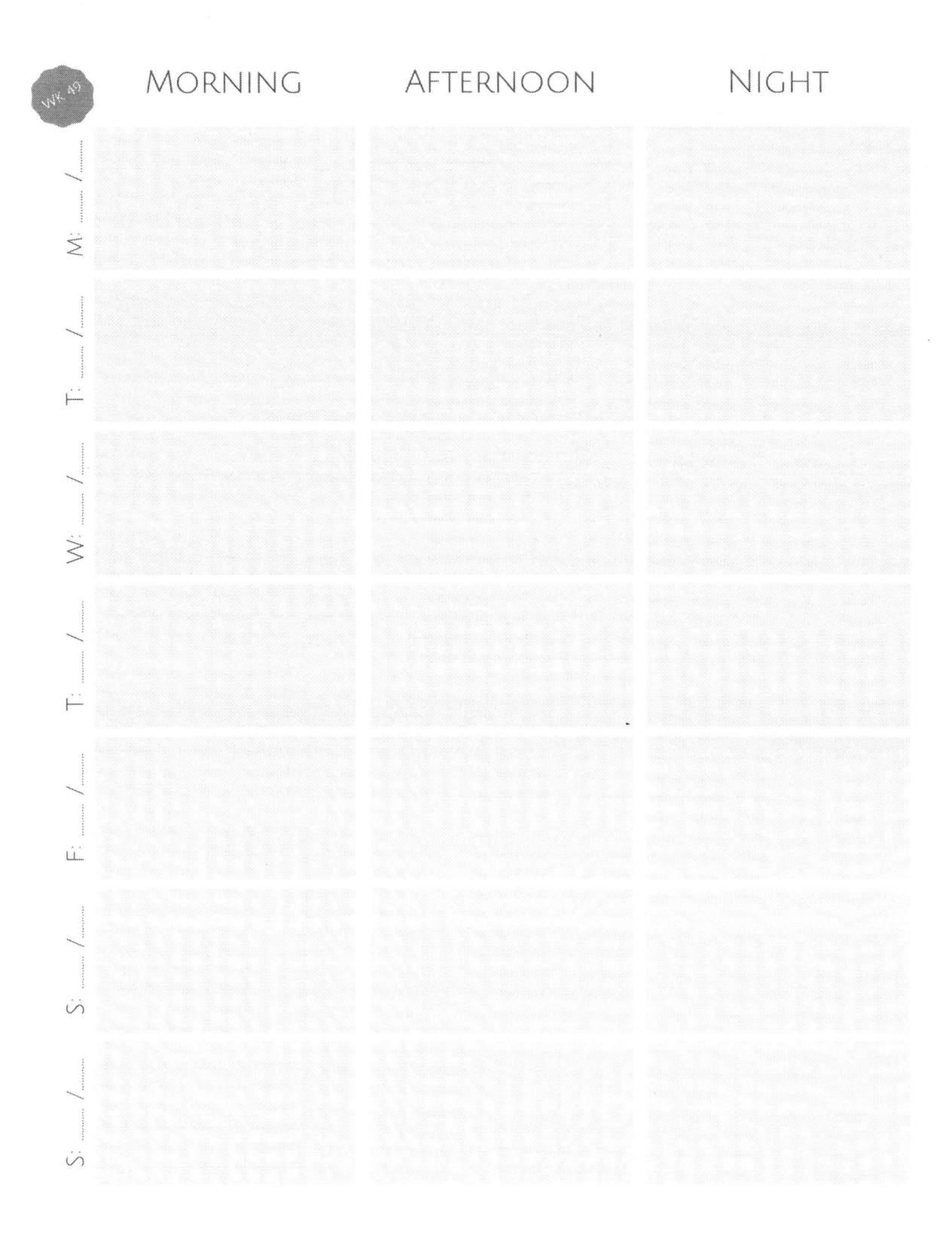

|  | MORNING | AFTERNOON | NIGHT |
|---|---|---|---|
| M: / | | | |
| T: / | | | |
| W: / | | | |
| T: / | | | |
| F: / | | | |
| S: / | | | |
| S: / | | | |

# WRITING PROMPT

*Each writing prompt is optional. If, for whatever reason, it does not speak to you, let it be. Who knows? It might make more sense to do the prompt later in the process.*

Some writers are in love with the rewriting and editing phases of the work, while other writers would love to run and hide when that time comes around.

Grab a piece of writing you're pretty happy with. Now rewrite your text while keeping the original version. Once you're done revising, compare the two pieces.

If you're feeling particularly bold this week, send both pieces to a critique partner or writing buddy without telling them which is the original and which is the 2.0 version. Just ask them which version they prefer and why. Now wait for the results.

# WEEK 50

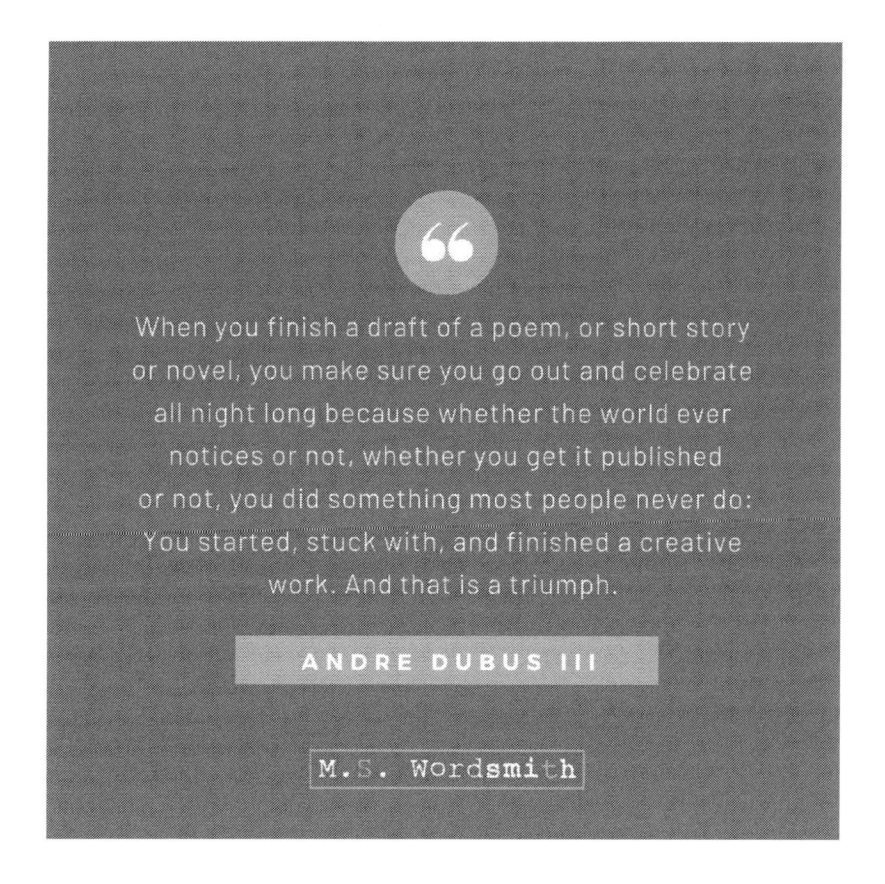

> When you finish a draft of a poem, or short story or novel, you make sure you go out and celebrate all night long because whether the world ever notices or not, whether you get it published or not, you did something most people never do: You started, stuck with, and finished a creative work. And that is a triumph.
>
> **ANDRE DUBUS III**

M.S. Wordsmith

## COME ON... YOU'RE ALMOST THERE!

DATE: _____

# Tracking

What goal(s) did you set for the past week?

Did you achieve your goal(s)?

WK 50

# Tracking

If yes, did you expect too little of yourself, or was your goal just right? If no, what prevented you from achieving it?

If you didn't reach your goals, what can you do next week to make sure you do?

If you picked an accountability partner last week, was this the right person? What worked and what didn't? Is there anything you'll want to do differently next week?

# Planning

What are your goals for the upcoming week?

Have another look. Are you sure this is realistic?
If not, what would be more realistic?

What can you do this week to make sure you achieve your goal(s)?

WK 50

# PLANNING

What smaller pieces can you break your goal(s) up into?
Once you're sure you can't break it down anymore, add the sub-goals to the calendar on the next page.

WK 50

|     | MORNING | AFTERNOON | NIGHT |
|-----|---------|-----------|-------|
| WK 50 |  |  |  |
| M: __ / __ |  |  |  |
| T: __ / __ |  |  |  |
| W: __ / __ |  |  |  |
| T: __ / __ |  |  |  |
| F: __ / __ |  |  |  |
| S: __ / __ |  |  |  |
| S: __ / __ |  |  |  |

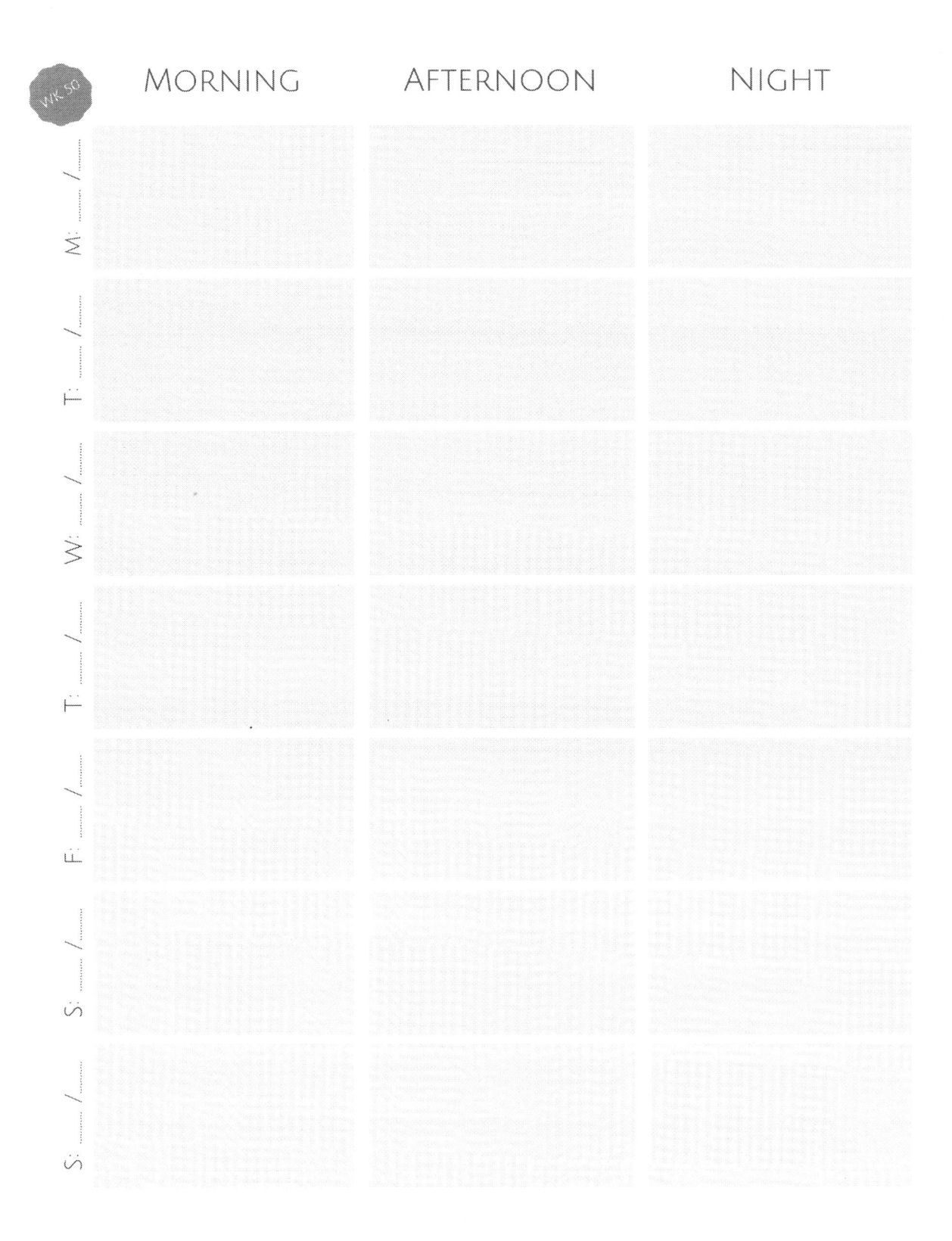

# WRITING PROMPT

*Each writing prompt is optional. If, for whatever reason, it does not speak to you, let it be. Who knows? It might make more sense to do the prompt later in the process.*

Do you celebrate your wins, no matter how small? Grab a notebook or open a new document on your computer and go back over the past forty-nine weeks. Write down your wins, your milestones, no matter how small. Really sit with it, and revel in how far you've come.

# Week 51

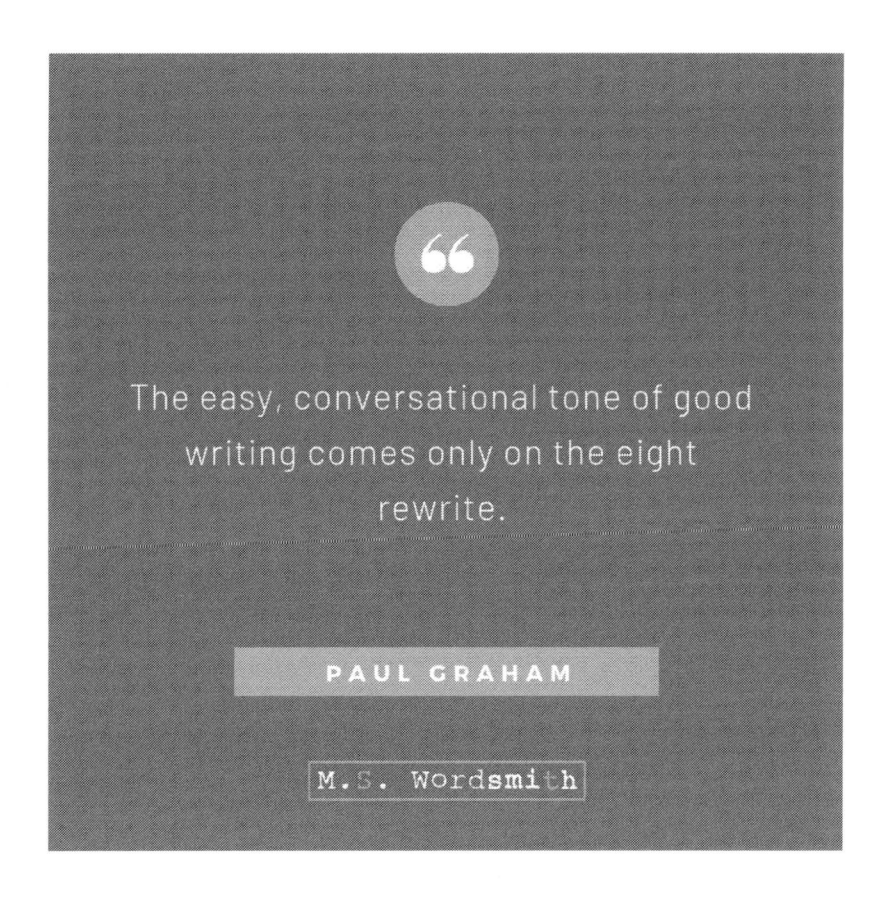

> The easy, conversational tone of good writing comes only on the eight rewrite.
>
> **PAUL GRAHAM**
>
> M.S. Wordsmith

DATE: ...........................................................

# Tracking

What goal(s) did you set for the past week?

Did you achieve your goal(s)?

WK 51

# TRACKING

If yes, did you expect too little of yourself, or was your goal just right? If no, what prevented you from achieving it?

If you didn't reach your goals, what can you do next week to make sure you do?

If you picked an accountability partner last week, was this the right person? What worked and what didn't? Is there anything you'll want to do differently next week?

# PLANNING

What are your goals for the upcoming week?

Have another look. Are you sure this is realistic?
If not, what would be more realistic?

What can you do this week to make sure you achieve your goal(s)?

WK 51

# PLANNING

What smaller pieces can you break your goal(s) up into?
Once you're sure you can't break it down anymore, add the sub-goals to the calendar on the next page.

WK 51

## WK 51

|  | Morning | Afternoon | Night |
|---|---|---|---|
| M: / / | | | |
| T: / / | | | |
| W: / / | | | |
| T: / / | | | |
| F: / / | | | |
| S: / / | | | |
| S: / / | | | |

# WRITING PROMPT

*Each writing prompt is optional. If, for whatever reason, it does not speak to you, let it be. Who knows? It might make more sense to do the prompt later in the process.*

Return to the piece of writing you revised during Week Forty-nine. Starting from the second version, rewrite this particular piece every single day for a week. As in Week Forty-nine, keep the different versions. At the end of the week, compare notes.

What do you notice about your writing? What strikes you the most?

# Week 52

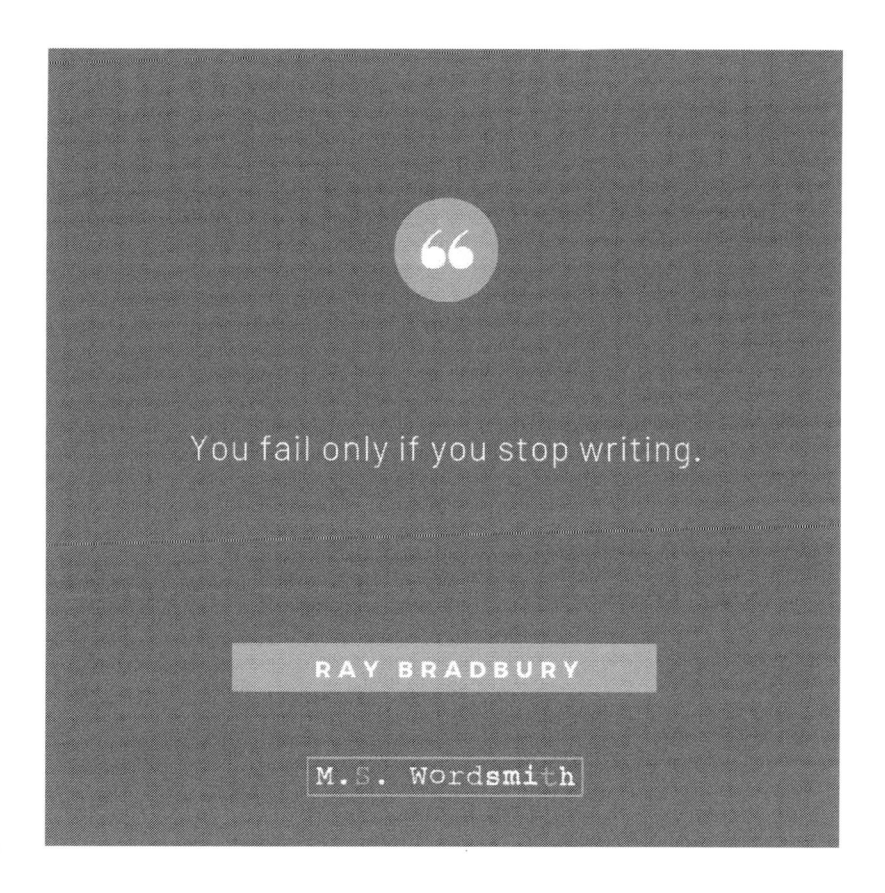

> You fail only if you stop writing.
>
> **RAY BRADBURY**

M.S. Wordsmith

ONLY ONE MORE WEEK TO GO!

DATE: ........................................................

# Tracking

What goal(s) did you set for the past week?

Did you achieve your goal(s)?

WK 52

# Tracking

If yes, did you expect too little of yourself, or was your goal just right? If no, what prevented you from achieving it?

If you didn't reach your goals, what can you do next week to make sure you do?

If you picked an accountability partner last week, was this the right person? What worked and what didn't? Is there anything you'll want to do differently next week?

# PLANNING

What are your goals for the upcoming week?

Have another look. Are you sure this is realistic?
If not, what would be more realistic?

What can you do this week to make sure you achieve your goal(s)?

# PLANNING

What smaller pieces can you break your goal(s) up into?
Once you're sure you can't break it down anymore, add the sub-goals to the calendar on the next page.

# WK 52

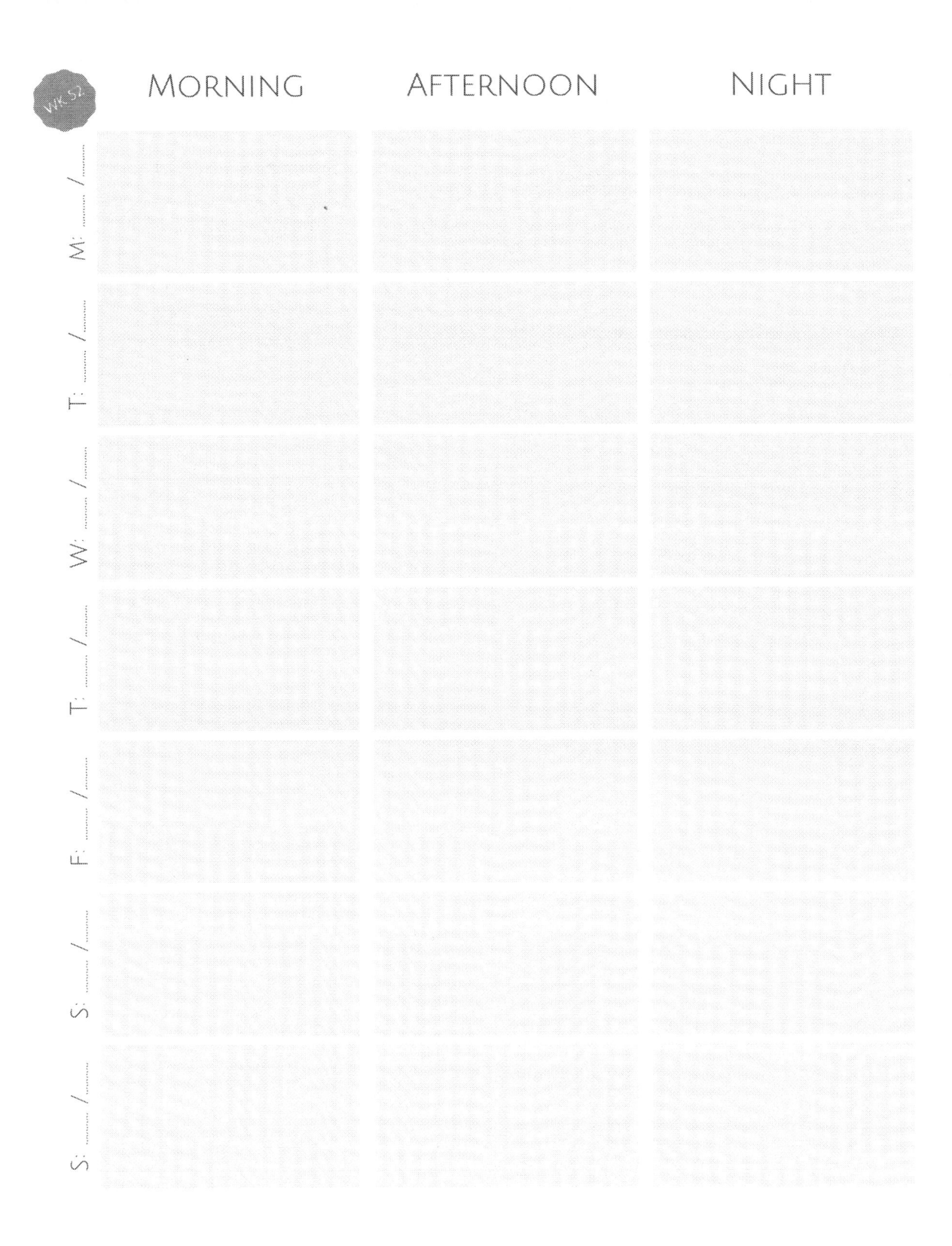

|  | MORNING | AFTERNOON | NIGHT |
|---|---|---|---|
| M: __/__ | | | |
| T: __/__ | | | |
| W: __/__ | | | |
| T: __/__ | | | |
| F: __/__ | | | |
| S: __/__ | | | |
| S: __/__ | | | |

# WRITING PROMPT

*Each writing prompt is optional. If, for whatever reason, it does not speak to you, let it be. Who knows? It might make more sense to do the prompt later in the process.*

Do you ever feel like giving up? What keeps you going?

Grab a piece of paper and write down the one reason you shouldn't quit (unless you can think of more, of course). Once you're done, put it somewhere you can see it daily (stick it to your computer screen, pin it to your wall, put it in your planner, wherever makes sense to you).

# Week 53

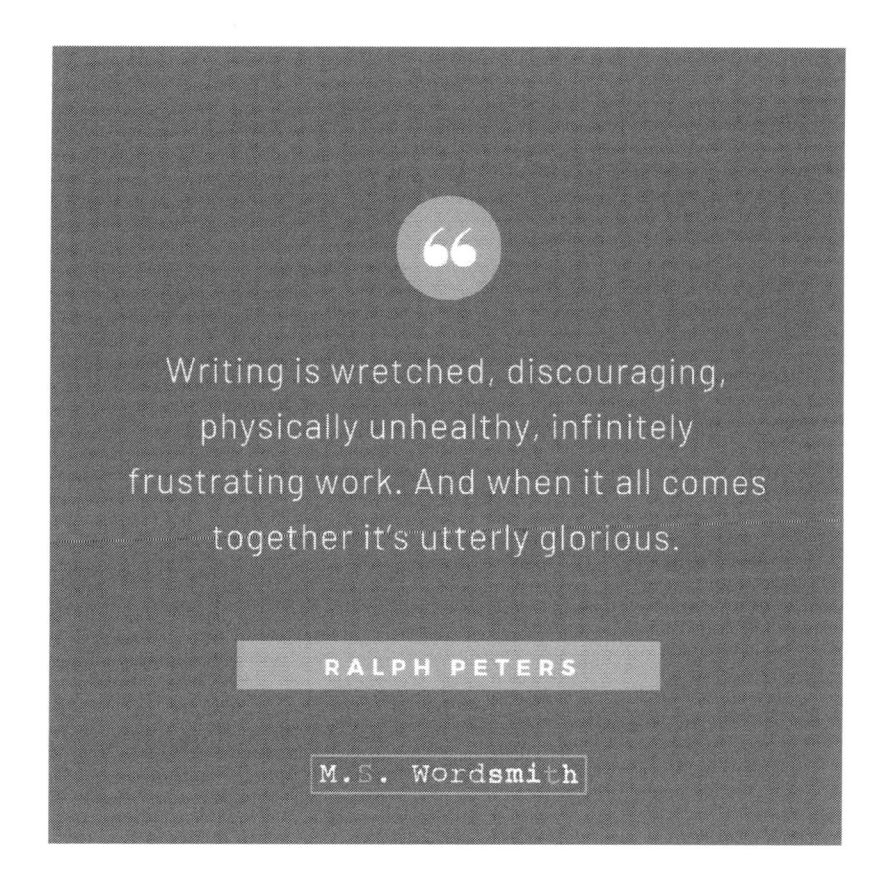

> Writing is wretched, discouraging, physically unhealthy, infinitely frustrating work. And when it all comes together it's utterly glorious.
>
> **RALPH PETERS**

M.S. Wordsmith

YOU MADE IT!

DATE: ....................................................

# Clarity

During Week One, you wrote down why you were first called to write. Over the past three months, have you been able to reconnect to that calling? Take a moment to reflect.

Over the past three months, have you been able to reconnect to how writing used to make you feel? There are no right or wrong answers here. Like the calling, your feelings about writing might have shifted. Take a moment to reflect on this as well.

# CLARITY

Looking back over the past three months, how did the act of writing make you feel? How did you feel right before you started, during, and once you were done?

Are you dealing with the same struggles and roadblocks you identified when we started this journey, or have they changed? If they have, what are you currently struggling with?

WK 53

# CLARITY

For each struggle and roadblock you are (still) dealing with, can you determine which are internal or external? Even if your list hasn't changed, still reflect on this. Something might very well have shifted in the meantime.

# CLARITY

For each struggle and roadblock, what do you think you need to overcome it? If you're still dealing with the same struggle(s) or roadblock(s), this doesn't mean you didn't make any progress. This is where you get to determine whether you did.

# Reflecting

Let's take a moment to reflect. When looking back on the past three months, what are you most grateful for?

What are the most significant lessons you have learned about yourself and your writing?

Did you achieve your 3-month goal(s)? If yes, (how) did you celebrate? If not, what steps could you take from this week onwards to ensure you reach your next 3-month goal(s)?

# Reflecting

*Now look at the year as a whole.*

When looking back on the past fifty-two weeks, what are you most grateful for?

What are the most significant lessons you have learned about yourself and your writing?

Did you achieve your 1-year goal(s)? If yes, (how) did you celebrate? If not, what steps could you take from this week onwards to ensure you reach your next 1-year goal(s)?

WK 53

# GOALS

*Now a whole year has passed, let's look at your long-term goals again. Is it time to adjust?*

Where do you want to be ten years from now? How are you going to celebrate?

In five years? How are you going to celebrate?

In three years? How are you going to celebrate?

In two years? How are you going to celebrate?

# GOALS

Where do you want to be in the next fifty-two weeks? How are you going to celebrate?

In nine months? How are you going to celebrate?

In six months? How are you going to celebrate?

In three months? How are you going to celebrate?

# Tracking

What goal(s) did you set for the past week?

Did you achieve your goal(s)?

WK 53

# Tracking

If yes, did you expect too little of yourself, or was your goal just right? If no, what prevented you from achieving it?

If you didn't reach your goals, what can you do next week to make sure you do?

If you picked an accountability partner last week, was this the right person? What worked and what didn't? Is there anything you'll want to do differently next week?

# PLANNING

*Because we both know this isn't over.*

What are your goals for the upcoming week?

Have another look. Are you sure this is realistic?
If not, what would be more realistic?

What can you do this week to make sure you achieve your goal(s)?

WK_53

# Planning

What smaller pieces can you break your goal(s) up into?
Once you're sure you can't break it down anymore, add the sub-goals to the calendar on the next page.

Wk 53

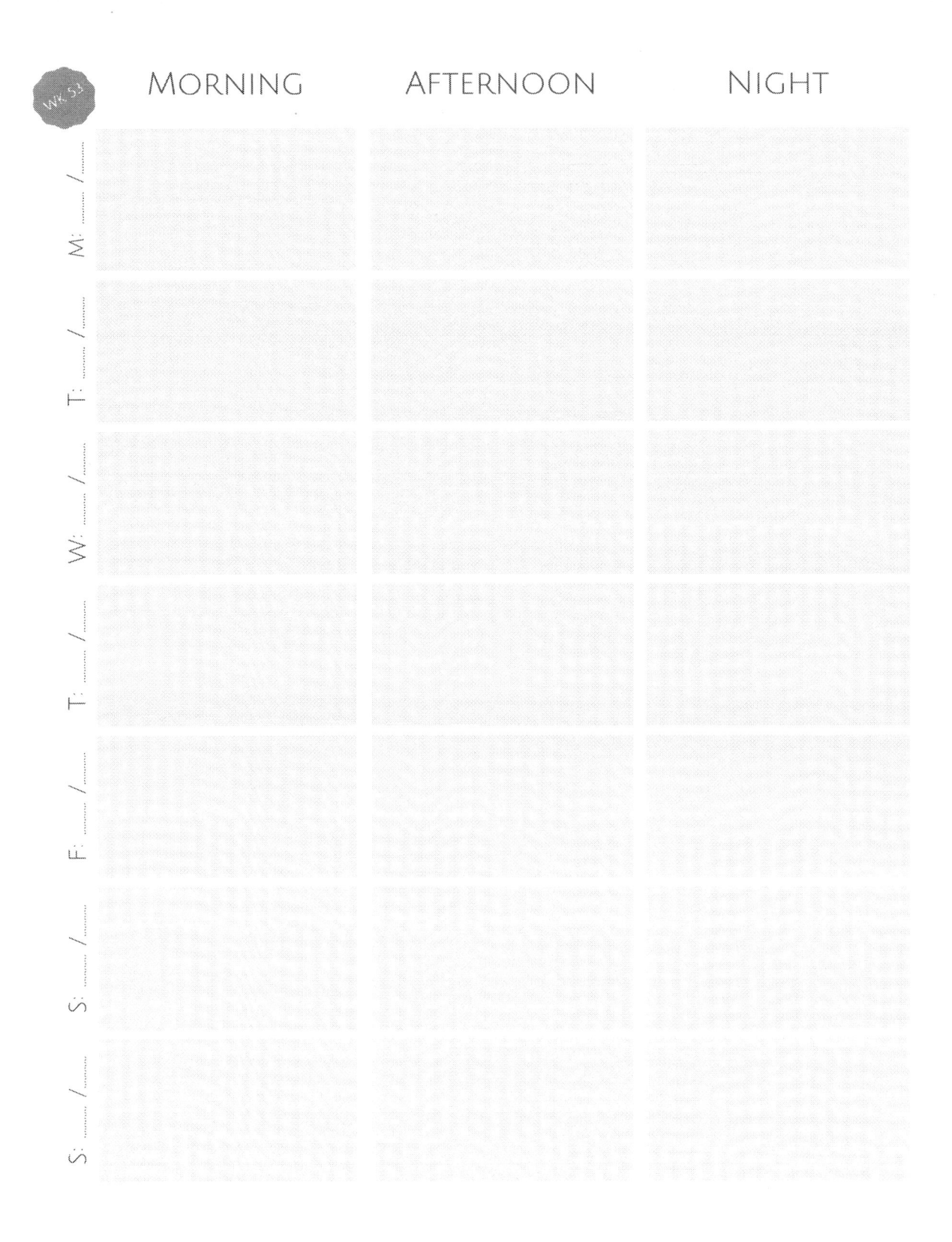

| | MORNING | AFTERNOON | NIGHT |
|---|---|---|---|
| M: __/__ | | | |
| T: __/__ | | | |
| W: __/__ | | | |
| T: __/__ | | | |
| F: __/__ | | | |
| S: __/__ | | | |
| S: __/__ | | | |

# Writing Prompt

*Each writing prompt is optional. If, for whatever reason, it does not speak to you, let it be. Who knows? It might make more sense to do the prompt later in the process.*

Look at the writing prompts of this past year. Which did you enjoy doing the most? Which were difficult to tackle? Which did you skip? There's still time to do them, if you'd like to.

Take a moment to reflect on what each writing prompt taught you about yourself and your writing. If you skipped any, take a moment to ask yourself why you might have decided to skip these. What does this tell you?

You!
Did! It!

One! Year!
Long!

How does it feel?

# How are you going to celebrate?

Write it down, then go do it!

# Goal Overview

| | GOAL(S) | MADE IT? |
|---|---|---|
| WK 1 | | |
| WK 2 | | |
| WK 3 | | |
| WK 4 | | |
| WK 5 | | |
| WK 6 | | |
| WK 7 | | |
| WK 8 | | |
| WK 9 | | |
| WK 10 | | |
| WK 11 | | |
| WK 12 | | |
| WK 13 | | |
| 3 MONTHS | | |

# Goal overview

## What did I learn?

WK 1
WK 2
WK 3
WK 4
WK 5
WK 6
WK 7
WK 8
WK 9
WK 10
WK 11
WK 12
WK 13
3 MONTHS

# Goal Overview

| | GOAL(S) | MADE IT? |
|---|---|---|
| WK 14 | | |
| WK 15 | | |
| WK 16 | | |
| WK 17 | | |
| WK 18 | | |
| WK 19 | | |
| WK 20 | | |
| WK 21 | | |
| WK 22 | | |
| WK 23 | | |
| WK 24 | | |
| WK 25 | | |
| WK 26 | | |
| 6 MONTHS | | |

# Goal overview

## What did I learn?

WK 14
WK 15
WK 16
WK 17
WK 18
WK 19
WK 20
WK 21
WK 22
WK 23
WK 24
WK 25
WK 26
6 MONTHS

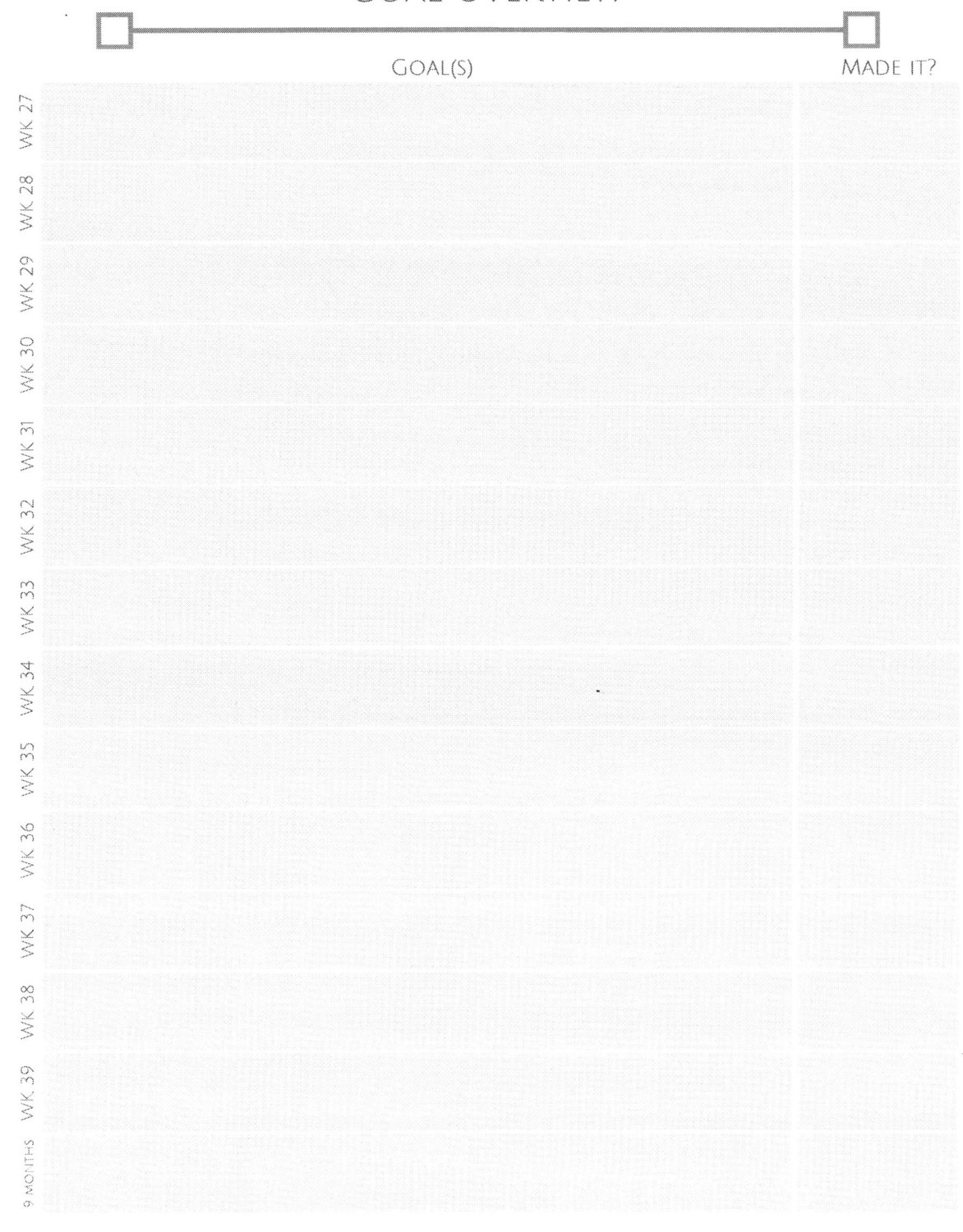

# Goal Overview

| | GOAL(S) | MADE IT? |
|---|---|---|
| WK 27 | | |
| WK 28 | | |
| WK 29 | | |
| WK 30 | | |
| WK 31 | | |
| WK 32 | | |
| WK 33 | | |
| WK 34 | | |
| WK 35 | | |
| WK 36 | | |
| WK 37 | | |
| WK 38 | | |
| WK 39 | | |
| 9 MONTHS | | |

# Goal Overview

## What did I learn?

WK 27
WK 28
WK 29
WK 30
WK 31
WK 32
WK 33
WK 34
WK 35
WK 36
WK 37
WK 38
WK 39
9 MONTHS

# Goal Overview

GOAL(S) | MADE IT?

| | |
|---|---|
| WK 40 | |
| WK 41 | |
| WK 42 | |
| WK 43 | |
| WK 44 | |
| WK 45 | |
| WK 46 | |
| WK 47 | |
| WK 48 | |
| WK 49 | |
| WK 50 | |
| WK 51 | |
| WK 52 | |
| 12 MONTHS | |

# Goal Overview

What did I learn?

| | |
|---|---|
| WK 40 | |
| WK 41 | |
| WK 42 | |
| WK 43 | |
| WK 44 | |
| WK 45 | |
| WK 46 | |
| WK 47 | |
| WK 48 | |
| WK 49 | |
| WK 50 | |
| WK 51 | |
| WK 52 | |
| 12 MONTHS | |

## IT GOES WITHOUT SAYING

that I would love to hear your story and how you got along.

If we aren't already in touch one way or the other, you can find me here:

MARIELLE@MSWORDSMITH.NL
MSWORDSMITH.NL
FACEBOOK.COM/MSWORDSMITH
INSTAGRAM.COM/MARIELLESSMITH

If you never want to miss an update about what I'm doing, you can sign up for my newsletter here:

MSWORDSMITH.NL/NEWSLETTER

I would also love for you to leave a review on Goodreads or where you purchased this book. Honest reviews are vital to our work being found and read.

# WANT MORE?

*There is no greater agony than bearing an untold story inside of you.*

Maya Angelou

Go to mswordsmith.nl/journal and get the second volume of the *52 Weeks of Writing Author Journal and Planner*.

Asking the same questions but offering fifty-two different writing quotes and prompts/exercises, the second volume is the perfect tool to keep your writing practice going.

# WANT MORE STILL?

Head over to mswordsmith.nl/starterkit and get my free Get Out of Your Own Way Starter Kit now.

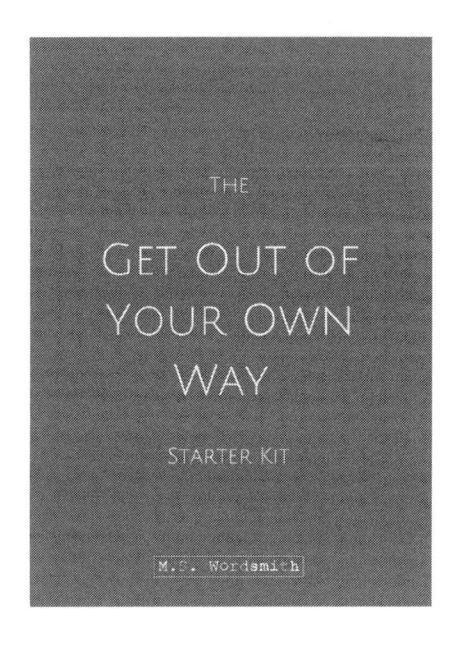

The Get Out of Your Own Way Starter Kit includes four different tools:

- An exercise on limiting beliefs,
- a monthly tracking and reflecting worksheet,
- a meditation on letting go of limiting beliefs,
- a tarot spread on creative roadblocks (from *Tarot for Creatives*),

and is yours when signing up to my newsletter.

## Acknowledgements

I would like to thank

my BETA team for working through multiple renditions of this journal and planner

my ARC TEAM for their brilliant feedback and for supporting all that I do

and ANDRI for making it easy to claim all the space I need to write